SUCCESS THROUGH POSITIVE THINKING

IS HALF FULL BETTER OR HALF EMPTY?

S.P. Sharma

V&S PUBLISHERS

Published by:

V&S PUBLISHERS

F-2/16, Ansari road, Daryaganj, New Delhi-110002
☎ 23240026, 23240027 • *Fax:* 011-23240028
Email: info@vspublishers.com • *Website:* www.vspublishers.com
Online Brandstore: *amazon.in/vspublishers*

Regional Office : Hyderabad
5-1-707/1, Brij Bhawan (Beside Central Bank of India Lane)
Bank Street, Koti, Hyderabad - 500 095
☎ 040-24737290
E-mail: vspublishershyd@gmail.com

Branch Office : Mumbai
Jaywant Industrial Estate, 1st Floor–108, Tardeo Road
Opposite Sobo Central Mall, Mumbai – 400 034
☎ 022-23510736
E-mail: vspublishersmum@gmail.com

ISBN 978-81-920796-4-6
Edition 2021

DISCLAIMER

While every attempt has been made to provide accurate and timely information in this book, neither the author nor the publisher assumes any responsibility for errors, unintended omissions or commissions detected therein. The author and publisher make no representation or warranty with respect to the comprehensiveness or completeness of the contents provided.
All matters included have been simplified under professional guidance for general information only without any warranty for applicability on an individual. Any mention of an organization or a website in the book by way of citation or as a source of additional information doesn't imply the endorsement of the content either by the author or the publisher. It is possible that websites cited may have changed or removed between the time of editing and publishing the book.
Results from using the expert opinion in this book will be totally dependent on individual circumstances and factors beyond the control of the author and the publisher.
It makes sense to elicit advice from well informed sources before implementing the ideas given in the book. The reader assumes full responsibility for the consequences arising out from reading this book. For proper guidance, it is advisable to read the book under the watchful eyes of parents/guardian. The purchaser of this book assumes all responsibility for the use of given materials and information.

Printed at : Param Offsetters, Okhla, New Delhi–110020

"The only real use of books is to make a man think for himself. If a book will not set one thinking, it is not worth shelf-room".

—William Lyon Phelps in
'Autobiography with Letters'

"Like the bee gathering honey from different flowers, the wise man accepts the essence of different Scriptures and sees only the good in all religions".

—Srimad Bhagavatram

"Every new discovery of science is a further revelation of the order that God has built into His universe".

—Warren Weaver

CONTENTS

INTRODUCTION

Humanity is one and indivisible. The problems and conflicts, the ideals and aspirations of the individual have essentially been the same in every part of the world and will continue to be so. If only the Battle of Waterloo was won on the playfields of Eton! The seeds of many a catastrophic war were sown in the minds of individuals, germinated there and the poisonous fruits of destruction scattered all over the world, directly or indirectly. We cannot view in isolation any event or state of affairs. If the world has progressed scientifically and technologically to an extent inconceivable a century ago, the ebb and flow of the moral calibre of man has become marked. The evidence of the horrible possibilities of the application of scientific inventions and discoveries to dreadfully destructive purposes is a pointer which should remind us that man's progress has been lopsided. The moral growth of the man has not matched his vast strides in other fields.* If man is to be saved from becoming a victim of his own lack of foresight, NOW is the time to subject ourselves to a searching introspection. If we want to build anew and make the world a safer place for generations to come, we must raise the individual's moral stature. We must assist him, advise him, guide him and elevate him.

In this task, it is common to imagine mistakenly that we ourselves are exempt from the follies and foibles of an

---

* "Our knowledge of science has clearly outstripped our capacity to control it. We have too many men of science; too few men of the Sermon on the Mount. The world has achieved brilliance without wisdom, power without conscience. Ours is a world of nuclear giants and ethical infants. We know more about war than we do about peace, more about killing than we do about living. This is our twentieth century's claim to distinction and progress."

—General Omar Bradley

imperfect civilisation and delude ourselves into thinking that this need for moral reappraisal and regeneration exists for others only. All of us have to learn and this naturally means an exchange of ideas and ideals. The word exchange is significant. In this context, it would be appropriate to recall the wise observations of Dr. Kenneth Walker:

> *"....it is my great veneration for the ancient culture of India, a culture in which, to my way of thinking, human thought and feeling have attained the highest level they have ever reached. So brilliant have India's past attainments been in the realms of religion and philosophy that I am convinced that she has a great contribution to make to present world thought and to the growth of world peace..... East and West have much to give each other and the closer the partnership we form in a stupendous effort to build a new and nobler world the better for us all."*
>
> ***—Introduction to "Women Saints of East and West."***

It is indeed trite to say that technological and economic power is not everything. People everywhere are reaping the consequences of a fast-paced life, being subjected to a variety of stresses and pressures. Preoccupation with science, technology, business and commerce leaves the average man little time for *thinking.* Indications everywhere in the world are that the average man acts on the spur of the moment and is hardly able to look beyond his nose; that he does not ponder or reflect on the verities of existence and is living at the surface. This lack of time and inclination to think, to reflect, is a dangerous portent. It breeds narrowness of mind which is the mother of hypocrisy, bigotry and intolerance and brings in its train needless misery to the individual. Carried to national and international level, the consequences have been truly disastrous.

Take the case of Hitler. His individual frustrations and narrow-mindedness, when they found congenial environment, flared up and erupted into a virulent militarism and a barbaric rejection of human values which engulfed the world by plunging it into a calamity of colossal magnitude. In America we found the obverse of the coin during the last century. The Civil War that raged between 1861 and 1865 was the result of the conscience of the enlightened and just section of the American nation throwing its weight strongly on the side of a cause that made them fight their own brethren. We should not forget that it was not the slaves fighting for their own emancipation. The conscience of the budding nation did not reconcile itself to the continuance of inequality between man and man. These sentiments are very truthfully reflected in the following lines by James Russell Lowell:

Men! whose boast it is that ye
Come of fathers brave and free,
If there breathe on earth a slave,
Are ye truly free and brave?
If you do not feel the chain
When it works a brother's pain,
Are you not base slaves indeed,
Slaves unworthy to be freed!

When vested interests thought there was no need for such a sacrifice, Civil War broke out. Because Lincoln, a man of broad vision, catholicity of views and humanitarian zeal was at the helm, the righteous cause triumphed. The wounds of the Civil War healed gradually and the nation marched ahead to take its place as the foremost democracy in the world.

The examples of Hitler and Lincoln are quoted here to underline the significance of the individual because leaders of men or nations symbolise the state of mind of the people of the nations concerned at the particular period of history.* As dramatically cautioned by a famous author, we cannot afford to underrate the *individual* power.

Apart from the need of the hour on the national and international plane, it is a fact that man ever hides beneath

---

*One of the people! born to be
Their curious epitome;

—R.H. Stoddard, "Abraham Lincoln"

his boisterous, and apparently non-chalant exterior, a burning desire to launch himself on a voyage to moral and spiritual regeneration and perfection. 'Men live not by bread alone.' The progress of the individual is slow no doubt, but sure, in spite of himself. Let us remind ourselves of the more important journey of man and render him what assistance we can on his way by providing milestones and sign-posts. Even if he had strayed, he can and must be brought back to the right track. If he is restless, if he is weary, let him rest awhile in the inns of religious, moral and spiritual consolations. Thus edified, let him rise and proceed apace, refreshed and encouraged!

❑❑❑

1

THIS PARADOXICAL WORLD

"For the wisdom of this world is foolishness with God".

I Corinthians 3 : 18.

"Suffer me not to judge according to the sight of the outward eye, nor to give sentence according to the hearing of the ears of men that know not what they are about; but to determine both of visible and spiritual matters with true judgement, and above all things, ever to seek Thy goodwill and pleasure.
"The senses of men are often wrong in their judgements, and the lovers of this world are deceived in loving visible things alone.
"How is man the better for being reputed greater by man?"

—The Imitation of Christ
(Book III Chapter 50)

CHANGING THE WAYS OF LIFE

For many of us, there seem to be no good reasons to change our ways of life. We are satisfied that we are living on the lines of the great majority of us. We are after health, wealth, sex and power. We are buoyant in fair weather and depressed and despondent in adversity. We go through life like a boat without a sail or rudder, downstream. We could not escape birth, we do not know why we are born. We have no choice but to live and drift. When great men make their appearance in our midst from time to time and, by their precept, demonstrate to us the supremacy of the spirit, we applaud them, admire them, glorify them, mostly because we are, at least we think we are, incapable of rising to their heights.

We have a great teacher in life: Enquiry. All progress, all learning is the result of enquiry. The more earnest the enquiry, the deeper the insight we gain. The more we ponder over things, the firmer become our convictions. If Newton had not enquired why the apple fell to the ground, how poor the world would have been. No doubt some other Newton could have made the discovery, but only after asking the same question!

Enquiry is necessary not only in the realm of knowledge of the physical sciences. It is an absolute must in day-do-day life if we are to gain an insight into the science of living.

Are we quite aware that we are banking too much on the reliability of our senses, mind and intellect in assessing the worth of worldly objects? Although we know vaguely that our senses like sight, touch and smell are liable to play us false, we continue to be guided entirely by them in deciding on any course of action. We are just content to receive information and knowledge second hand even where we should exercise independent judgement and thought. Why? Because we are busy living our little lives and there is less room for enquiry and reasoning.

WORLDLY VALUES AND THINGS

Moreover, we are being guided in every walk of life by popular notions and conventions. If you feel that 'love is a many splendoured thing', it is because from the time we could understand something about it, we have been conditioned by the books we read, the films we see and the stories we are told, to think on those lines. Wealth is a great blessing to be accumulated by all means and poverty a curse and therefore to be banished. Education makes our mind grow and expand. Sickness is something obnoxious which is to be prevented and cured. All these ideas are basically correct, no doubt. But, as they say, there are two sides to a coin. Every aspect of life is almost a paradox. As a matter of fact, this world of ours is bristling with paradoxes. At every step we are confronted with them which shatter the seeming finality of worldly values and things.

Long ago St. Francis of Assissi said: "It is in giving that we receive, it is in pardoning that we are pardoned and *it is in dying that we are born to everlasting life"*. But, then, religion and religious men have seemed to speak in a language that has always been strange and obscure to worldly men and women.

For all of us, youth is the spring of life, 'to be young is very heavenly' and old age is the gloomy evening of life, the verge of the dark night that is death. Yet Robert Browning wrote:

"Grow old along with me!
The best is yet to be,
The last of life for which the
first was made."

And Hervey Allen, in "Anthony Adverse" says: "The only time you really live fully is from thirty to sixty"—that is, exactly after you cease to be youthful.

After the ravages of two World Wars, when statesmen of the world were raking their brains to explore ways to a lasting peace, read what Voltaire in his 'Candidate' says: "In those towns which seem to enjoy the blessings of peace and where the arts flourish, men suffer more from envy, cares and anxieties than a besieged town suffers from the scourges of war, for secret vexations are much more cruel than public miseries." It is common knowledge that, in war-time, people of a nation sink their differences, make sacrifices for others and great acts of courage, selflessness and heroism are witnessed. Would Winston Churchill have come to be ranked among the world's greatest men but for his role in World War II?

If poets and novelists, too, seem to you to live in and speak from some other world, let us see what more mundane people of eminence have unravelled.

These are days of calories, balanced diet and nutrition. But the great Napoleon is reported to have held that 'however little a man may eat, he always eats too much. One can get ill from over-eating, but never from under-eating.' Good old Ben Franklin, who died full of years and honours and who had known both poverty and affluence in his life, went a step further. Recalling his younger days, he wrote in his Autobiography: "Living on meals which often were no more than a biscuit or a slice of bread, a handful of raisins or a tart from the pastry-cook's and a glass of water, I made the greater progress in my studies *from that greater clearness of head and quicker apprehension which usually attend temperance in eating and drinking."*

Speaking again of Napoleon, the triumphant hero of a hundred battles, who swore by the way of the sword (and, incidentally, perished by it!), proclaimed when in exile: "Force is no remedy, the spirit of man is greater than the sword." "Do you know", he said, "What amazes me more than all else? The impotence of force to organise anything. There are only two powers in the world: the spirit and the sword. In the long run the sword will always be conquered by the spirit." Then again, "War is an anachronism; some day victories will be won without cannon and without bayonets." The words of Napoleon proved prophetic: India gained her independence against the might of the mightiest of empires the non-violent way under the leadership of Mahatma Gandhi. Incidentally, it is interesting to recall that Gandhi handsomely acknowledged his indebtedness to Henry David Thoreau for the novel idea of passive resistance and soul-force.

But coming to more modern times, when one of the attractions of being rich is the additional care which it will enable us to bestow upon our children, child specialist, Dr. Josephine Baker says: "Children of wealthy parents, though often overfed, are as often undernourished and being too carefully guarded against contagion, establish no immunity and are prey to every germ."

Again, who would think that ill-health and disease have any beneficial effects on one's body? But Dr. Martin-Gumpert, M.D. avers that 'disease, by forcing the body to strengthen its defences, may contribute to increased vitality.'

PERSONALITY TRAITS & EDUCATION

How far does higher education improve our personality? Dr. Henry C. Link, the famous American Psychiatrist, after extensive studies, made these startling discoveries: "That in personality traits, people with practically no education equal college graduates; that the people who have the highest scholastic intelligence are just as likely as not to be lowest; those who are lowest in intelligence tests are just as likely as not to rank highest; that although the personality of some students improves during the high school and college ages, that of others deteriorates, so that the net result is zero. In other words, *there is no average improvement of personality due to education.*"

Have you ever regretted that you are not a brilliant intellectual? You do not seem to have lost much in the light of Dr. Link's findings and assertions: "The more intellectual the man, the wider his range of ideas, the more danger he is in putting gods of temporary expedience before the God of everlasting values."

Note yet another significant conclusion of the same celebrated psychiatrist, exposing the futility of the exclusive pursuit of scientific and technological knowledge which, if it has added to our physical comfort, has certainly not reduced our mental restlessness. "There can be no solution of life's deeper problems, no increased happiness for the individual, through the development of greater scientific knowledge alone. More science only adds more confusion. Unless the sciences are integrated and subordinated to the homely facts of every-day living, they will destroy rather than liberate the minds which created them. This integration must come from without the sciences themselves, it is not inherent in them and it is not a subject for scientific proof. It must come from a faith, a belief in certain values of life which is fundamental and which no logic can displace."

Now do you feel a little less sure of the ground on which we stand on temporal matters? This is the first step in our journey towards a saner sense of values, leading us gradually to the awareness of the Kingdom of God.

❑❑

2

THE SECRET OF SELF-GENERATING JOY

"The essence of philosophy is that a man should so live that his happiness shall depend as little as possible on external things."

—Epictetus

"A happy life must be to a great extent a quiet life, for it is only in an atmosphere of quiet that true joy can live."

—Bertrand Russell

FEELING OF HAPPINESS

"Oh, I am so happy!", says Mary. "Why, what happened?", asks her friend. "Last night", replies Mary, "John did what it seemed almost impossible—he took me in his arms and asked me to be his wife."

"I am happy that I accepted your invitation to dine with you", says Mr. Gourmet. "The food was excellent, my appetite no less so. It is a long time since I had sampled such cuisine and wine."

"Thank God, I am relaxed and happy," says a mother. "My little Tom was hovering between life and death with an attack of diphtheria. I had given up all hopes. Then the miracle happened: he tided over the crisis and gradually regained normal health."

Could you discern anything common in the "happiness" felt by the three different individuals under different sets of circumstances? "Happiness" as generally used is an omnibus word. In one case it is simply the prospect of future felicity.

In another, it is used to express mere sensual pleasure or mental satisfaction. In the third, it indicates the relief felt when a danger recedes. Since an appreciation of the true nature of happiness is an essential step in resolving some of the endless conflicts of worldly existence, it would not be a mere intellectual exercise if we devoted a little of our time to the examination of its characteristics.

Though man's primary concern is to satisfy natural needs like hunger and thirst and protect himself from the forces of nature like rain and storm, and he expends a great deal of his energy in satisfying these basic needs of life, yet he has another distinct and more imperious urge—the pursuit of happiness.* As psychologist William James has said "How to gain, how to keep, how to recover happiness is in fact for most men at all times the secret motive of all they do, and of all they are willing to endure." Unfortunately, pleasure is invariably mistaken for happiness.

FULFILMENT OF PLEASURE

Now, what is pleasure? It is nature's compensation for man's exertion to meet his biological needs. It may be even a bait. Whenever he feels a want, man has to exert himself and in the course of satisfaction, derive a certain enjoyment—an agreeable sensation—which may be termed pleasure. When he is hungry, he has to seek and prepare food. When he eats, not only is his hunger assuaged, but he derives a certain pleasurable feeling also. Thus the very act of fulfilling a biological need, gives rise to pleasure. Nature originally must have meant the pleasures of sex to be a bait to induce men and women to undertake the responsibility of parenthood and thus help the perpetuation of species.

This link between natural needs—the exertion required for their fulfilment and the pleasure he derives in the satisfaction of want, is often lost sight of. The result is the hunting of

---

*O Happiness! our being's end and aim good, Pleasure, Ease, Content!
Whate'er thy name; That something still, which prompts the eternal sigh,
For which we bear to live or dare to die.

—**Alexander Pope,** *On Happiness*

pleasure for pleasure's sake and a divorce between the need and its satisfaction. For example, instead of realising that he takes food to satisfy his hunger, man may, so to say, put the cart before the horse, by seeking food as a source of enjoyment. On the same basis, the advent of modern contraceptives has highlighted the relegation, and even defeat of Nature's purpose by which man indulges in sex for pleasure instead of progeny.

Mankind lives a hand-to-mouth existence. Constant effort alone can keep the world going. Primitive man expended the same day the food he procured and had to go hunting daily to meet his food needs. Later his ingenuity enabled him to set apart something for the morrow. By and large, the hand-to-mouth existence continues, but there is a great deal of difference today. What with the division of labour and progress of industry and commerce and the introduction of the common denominator of value, money, every man need not himself produce the goods he consumes. As a result, while the object of his daily labour, in whatever sphere it be, still is to earn so that the basic needs can be met, the pursuit of pleasure has grown in intensity. The divorce between a need and its satisfaction is complete and now the accent is almost exclusively on pleasure.

An analysis would reveal that pleasure is generally caused by the contact of the senses with objects of their agreeability. Smell, taste, hearing, vision and touch yield pleasure as long as the respective organs are in immediate contact with objects agreeable to them—perfumes, delicious food, sweet sounds like music, pleasant sights and so on. The pleasure of the particular type ceases when the organ or sense loses the contact.

Here we must make a slight digression. In all these things, the role the mind plays should not be lost sight of. A sense organ comes in contact with an object agreeable or pleasant to it. But the mind must co-operate and take cognizance of it, otherwise the pleasure or its opposite sensation is not registered. It is not an unusual thing in our daily life to look and yet not see, eat and still not know the taste. This happens when the mind is straying or busy with something else. This phenomenon has a very important bearing in the moulding of our lives deliberately.

The pursuit of sense-pleasure has its curious reaction: It gives rise to likes and dislikes—liking for the pleasant and dislike for the opposite, that is, what is not pleasant, less pleasant and positively unpleasant which can broadly be classified as pain.

Yet another chain reaction is generated by the hankering for pleasure. Eagerness for it creates impatience, thwarting of its attainment causes anger and frustration, the desire of pleasure itself creates an insensibility or disability to perceive things in the proper light, which may be termed 'delusion'. Again, rivalry and conflict result when a single object is sought after by more than one person. The possession of objects of pleasure causes pride and miserliness. It will also be clear that pleasure is a subjective experience with selfishness as its keynote.

Moreover, there is a certain uncertainty in the sensation itself which the object gives rise to. The same object may be the cause of pleasure or pain under different circumstances. Warmth on a wintry morning provides comfort, but on a summer day, causes positive discomfort.

DEALING WITH PLEASURES

We have so far been dealing with purely sensual pleasures. There is another variety, namely mental pleasure or the pleasure of emotion. We term love, humour etc., as pleasant emotions and feelings like hatred, anger and greed, as unpleasant emotions. Mental pleasure also partakes largely of the shortcomings of the sensual kind, but in a way it is superior to the other.

We can go a step further and define a third kind of pleasure: intellectual pleasure—the elation that certain convictions, as distinguished from emotions, give rise to. And its opposite: intellectual pain. An example of intellectual pleasure is Marxism or Socialism as a creed in which Marxists and Socialists delight.

Let us now draw out the common characteristics of the three kinds of pleasures:

(1) Their need for contact with something agreeable, i.e., dependence on external objects.
(2) The various undesirable reactions that attend the pursuit of pleasure for its own sake at different stages.
(3) The inability of objects to yield pleasure uniformly under all conditions.
(4) Pleasure breeds selfishness and is in turn bred by it.

We come presently to the last, and perhaps the most important, attribute of pleasure. When is pleasure felt? When the 'hunger' for pleasure is satisfied. To put it in another, more clear way, a man's equanimity is disturbed first when he thinks he should have a particular thing and feels that he can regain it (equanimity) only when that hunger is satisfied. So he sets out to get that sensation or object and getting it, feels 'pleasure'. A smoker becomes restless as soon as the thought of a smoke comes to his mind and he will regain his composure only when he consumes a cigarette. He satisfies that craving and thereby derives pleasure.

This point is well brought out in the argument between Socrates and the sophist. Socrates stood for felicity as the supreme happiness and the sophist for desiring and getting. The sophist said that Socrates' felicity was that of a block of wood; whereupon Socrates said his antagonist's bliss was that of a man who had itch, who did nothing but scratch!

So another basic characteristic of pleasure is that *it stems from a feeling of inadequacy of some sort.* In the words of Adler, "Every voluntary act begins with a feeling of inadequacy whose resolution proceeds towards a condition of satisfaction, of repose, of totality." Inadequacy is thus at the bottom of pleasure which is merely eliminating that insufficiency. *It could be seen that pleasure cannot stand on its own legs.* This is another important factor.

Let us now examine the nature of *happiness* which is a more difficult thing to comprehend. Oriental mystics and philosophers have devoted considerable attention to it and carried out exhausting research in the laboratory of life to ascertain its nature. As a result they have concluded that happiness is the true nature of the soul. (A more appropriate word for happiness would be "Joy" or "Bliss") That is, by nature man is happy and as long as he is not invaded by desire-born disturbances, he is in a state of joy which *needs no support and is its own foundation as well as superstructure.*

The last statement can be elucidated somewhat satisfactorily, the statement that joy is our real, original true nature.* How? Let me explain. Suppose you are just relaxing in a chair in your garden one fine morning, sipping a soft drink, basking in the pleasant warm sunshine. There is no reason for you to be particularly happy nor any to be unhappy. In other words, you have a clear choice to be either happy or unhappy. Which would you choose if you are a more or less normal individual? Would you refuse to be happy because you do not have a particular cause to be happy? On the contrary, would you not assert that you would be a fool indeed if you denied yourself joy for the very reason that there is nothing about which you should mope?

JOY—THE INEFFABLE PEACE

In contrast to pleasure, joy is independent of any external object or internal emotion. It is simply the state of equilibrium. It seeks nothing and gives man the only thing that is worthwhile in life: JOY itself! Once you have grasped this secret, JOY UNLIMITED is yours.

Man's comprehension of joy is as an ineffable peace—'the peace that passeth understanding'. The body, the mind, the senses, the intellect are all at rest—there is a lightness, a buoyancy which does not goad you to action. Then comes the perception of the existence of the soul as different from, and superior to the body, mind and intellect.

---

* "Man is more himself, man is more manlike, when joy is the fundamental thing in him.... joy is the uproarious labour by which all things live."

—G.K. Chesterton

This description of happiness, joy, may seem to indicate that it is beyond the compass of ordinary run of individuals. Not necessarily so, because there is an element of joy or happiness in pleasure itself. It may be said that pleasure is happiness in patches. When we feel happy (even in patches) we are having a glimpse of that One Solid Happiness.

"Kings lick the earth whereof the fair are made,
For God hath mingled in the dusty earth
A draught of Beauty from His choicest cup,
'T is that, *fond lover—not these lips of clay—*
Thou are kissing with a hundred ecstasies,
Think, then, what must it be when undefiled!

—Jalal-al-Din Rumi

"All that is sweet, delightful, and amiable in this world, in the serenity of the air, the fineness of seasons, the joy of light, the melody of sounds, the splendour of precious stones, is nothing else but Heaven breaking through the veil of this world, manifesting itself in such a degree and darting forth in such variety so much of its own nature."

—William Law

"Every moment we are enjoying the Absolute Bliss, though covered up, misunderstood and caricatured. Wherever there is any blessing, blissfulness or joy, even the joy of the thief in stealing, it is that Absolute Bliss coming out; only it has become obscured, muddled up, as it were, with all sorts of extraneous conditions and misunderstood."

—Vivekananda

Another quotation, one from that modern mystic, Thomas Merton, also brings out clearly by implication the existence of joy independent of, infinitely superior to and quite different from pleasure:

"Do not look for rest in any pleasure because you were created for joy and if you do not

know the difference between pleasure and joy you have not yet begun to live."

As already explained, most of us are unaware of real happiness and there is a striking unanimity in the mistake and confusion of pleasure for happiness. The exposition of the nature of pleasure as distinct from happiness attempted in the foregoing should enable us to strive to "seek" happiness. It will take considerable practice to be aware of and enjoy the bliss independent, the joy unlimited. As a matter of fact, religion and particularly meditation and prayer, are meant to lead us on to the practice of the art of being happy, joyous. By detaching our body, mind and intellect from their moorings in sense-and-desire-born hankering for pleasure, by steadying them and fixing them on a sublime concept, we are indeed trained to discover the true nature of our being which is joy, bliss.

The common conception of religion and philosophy as a negation or denial of everything that is naturally enjoyable also results from this confusion of pleasure for happiness. The distilled wisdom of humanity, which religion in essence is, seeks to wean man away from ephemeral, transcient satisfaction and lead him on to a sustained, sound and substantial enjoyment of true joy, bliss, happiness.

The description given above may perhaps be taken as representing purely the oriental view-point. Therefore it would indeed be fitting to quote here, Dr. Earl L. Douglass:

"Happiness is the gift of God. The reason so many people fail to find happiness is that they do not know where to look for it. They think they will find it in wealth; but money alone never made anyone happy. They think they will find it in ease; but freedom from responsibility produces restlessness more often than it produces happiness. They seek after social position, thrilling types of pleasure, places of honour; and often they try to find happiness in some gross indulgence.

They are on the wrong road. So long as they live they will never find happiness along any of *these highways; and that for the simple reason that happiness is in our hearts,* or it is nowhere. It is a condition of the inner life not of the outer. Its chief characteristic is peace, not possession; contentment, not ambition; love and sacrifice, not pleasure and indulgence. It comes when a man stops fighting the universe and rests himself in the hand of the One who has made the universe and still manages it—when he stops trying to find happiness in the world and looks for it in his own heart."*

Summing up, we shall indicate here how to put the knowledge gained in this chapter to practical use. When there is no particular reason to be happy or unhappy, let us lift our state of contentment deliberately to a high level, and reflect joy—think, act and speak joyously. By conscious practice of joy, being joyful becomes our normal state instead of being depressed or merely indifferent or inert. Thus when there is a definite reason for being more happy, it will lift you to greater heights. In moments of distress (which we cannot avoid till we are firmly established in the kingdom of God), by maintaining a cheerful attitude, even if it be an assumed one, it will not take you too much to the bottom. Let us give ourselves a new slogan: "LET US EVER BE JOYOUS—FOR NO OTHER REASON EXCEPT THAT IT IS OUR TRUE NATURE—JOY IS OUR BIRTHRIGHT". And secondly,—this should be more important—let us set apart at least half-an-hour of our leisure time daily for the practice of meditation and prayer, a few useful hints you will find in a subsequent chapter bearing that title.

❑❑

---

* If solid happiness we prize,
Within our breast this jewel lies;
And they are fools who roam;
The world hath nothing to bestow,
From our ownselves, our bliss must flow,
And that dear hut—our home.

—Nathaniel Cotton (1707-1788)
—THE FIRESIDE.

3

WORK, THE EMANCIPATOR—I

"Every act rewards itself first in our own soul, then in circumstance. People call the circumstance retribution."

—Emerson

"Nothing can work me damage except myself; the harm that I sustain I carry with me and never am a real sufferer but by my own fault."

—St. Bernard

"Activity is the only road to knowledge."

—G. Bernard Shaw

"Blessed is the man who has found his work. Let him ask no other blessedness."

—Thomas Carlyle

"One of the most durable satisfactions in life is to lose oneself in one's work.... One of the sovereign cures for unhealthy fears is action."

—Harry Emerson Fosdick

"It is through work, rather than play alone, that young people can avoid the physical and moral flabbiness which comes from idleness, and toughen their spiritual muscles sufficiently to carry the responsibilities of adult citizenship."

—Judge William G. Long

PUTTING THE CART BEFORE THE HORSE

A child is ill—very ill. It is rushed by its parent to a nearby doctor who is a stranger as the family physician is just then out of town. He does what his medical knowledge and experience dictate, to save the life of the child. But by next morning the child is dead. The parent is in agony. He is assailed by various doubts; did he do the right thing in taking the child to an unknown doctor? Was it the victim of wrong diagnosis and consequent incorrect treatment? Would the child have lived had it been rushed to a hospital where better attention would have been possible? Had he been guilty of an unwise action? Could the death of the child have been due to it?

Let us take another instance. I had a friend who was employed in the city. He had a cousin in the village who wanted a change. My friend got him down to the city and fixed him up on a job in a workshop. A week later, there was an accident. An iron girder collapsed and crashed to the shop floor. The cousin of my friend who was working directly underneath, was instantaneously killed! You can very well imagine the feelings of my friend—and those of the parents of the dead man. Would he not have lived peacefully in the village if he had not been brought to the city?

Now, under such tragic circumstances, what solace have science and technology to offer? Consolation lies purely on how and what one thinks. You will agree that the most intelligent and practical attitude to take would be to look at the whole thing this way: "I did what I thought was best then—the result is not in my hands." In fact, Abraham Lincoln, when crushed by the unbearable weight of the responsibility of taking a momentous decision, was reported to have done exactly the same thing. "I told God that I had done all that I could and that now the result was in His hands; that if this country was to be saved, it was because He so willed it! The burden rolled off my shoulders. My intense anxiety was relieved and in its place came a great trustfulness". These were his words.

Instead of applying such thinking to an isolated incident, or only after something has happened, would you consider it impractical and escapist if one uniformly took up this attitude: "I shall do everything as best as I can—to the best of my ability and judgement. I shall not be unduly exercised if the result did not turn out to be exactly what I had anticipated, nor shall I be exultant if my efforts were crowned with phenomenal success"?

Unfortunately, we always put the cart before the horse. From the start we attach ourselves passionately to the result.* We mobilise all our resources for the attack. We get tense. We work anxiously for the result. Doubt assails us as we are not sure of success. Thus all the joy that should normally be experienced in an endeavour undertaken in a relaxed, peaceful manner, is lost. Till the end, there is anxiety about the expected result. If the end is not a success—crash! And we are crushed. All the trouble and anxiety, we think, are justified only if the efforts end in achievement. We have to undertake work (another word for effort, endeavour) in our daily life. Work of various types—some 'important,' others 'not so important,' some of short duration, some time-consuming. The results expected are not of the same magnitude in all cases. Still the process is the same. Therefore our approach or attitude to *all* work has to be uniform.

That does not mean that we are indifferent. Only we avoid stress, tension. We cannot expect always to meet with success and the resulting elation. We cannot hope to enjoy only the pleasant part and avoid the unpleasant. One or the other is always around the corner. It is obvious that to be prepared for *both* is the only sensible and rational way to maintain equanimity. Is that indifference?

---

*"As a nation we are prone to think altogether too much in terms of results. I remember, several years ago, when I was an archery enthusiast, studying a manual of Japanese archery which I picked up in Yokohama and had translated. Under the Japanese system of marking, an arrow in the bull's eye was good for only 50 per cent on the score board. The *manner* in which the archer conformed to the traditional legends of the sport, the form with which he released the arrow, counted for the other 50 per cent.

"In American archery, a man could lie on his back, pull the bow with his feet, release the arrow with his teeth, get the arrow in the bull's eye and still the shot would count for a 100 per cent.

"We worship results."

—Erle Stanley Gardner in 'The Court of Last Resort'

WE REAP ONLY WHAT WE SOW

We have heard a lot about ends and means, sometimes of the end justifying the means. When we do not attach ourselves so passionately to the result, it can safely be assumed that there will not be unhesitating resort to undesirable means. Is that not commonsense?

As you sow, so you reap. That is pretty clear. Yet we do see in our lives many instances where the harvest does not seem to be proportionate to the crops sown. Small efforts sometimes are rewarded with unusual success. Very hard and sincere efforts do at times go in vain. Why should this be so? Contrary to popular notion, results are not *directly* proportional to actions There are various forces at work to neutralise a direct result. That is not to say that every action does not have an exclusive result all its own. For example, Bill Clinton was elected President of the United States of America, defeating his rival, George Bush. As can easily be seen, this is rather a culmination of a series or chain of actions, not only Mr. Clinton's but of several others, each one of which by itself could not put Mr. Clinton in the white House. It is also...... extremely difficult, or even impossible, to pinpoint which action attracted which result.

As already mentioned, we are convinced that we reap only what we sow. Naturally so! In the inimitable language of the Bible, 'do men gather grapes of thorns, or figs of thistles? Even so every good tree bringeth forth good fruit; but a corrupt tree bringeth forth evil fruit.' In this analogy, every deed has a more or less definite fruit. It is also clear that good deeds beget good results and bad ones, bad results. But here again, good and bad are relative terms. It is not unlikely that something bad might result out of a "good" deed. Strange? Suppose you "helped" a friend of yours with a ten dollar bill which he asked for as a loan. With that he buys some narcotic drug and launches himself on a career as a drug-addict. What has been the result of your "good" deed, your "help"?

There is another aspect to the problem. All events have a cause-and-effect relationship in them. An action is at once a cause and an effect. A tree has "caused" the seed, and the seed in turn is going to cause a tree. Which started first, the tree or the seed?

To avoid good or bad results, one might say that one will abstain from *all* actions. Is it possible? The world will come to an end directly if everyone abstained from work!

Work, therefore we all have to. Work is not or should not be, a curse because it is a must.

> *"The word 'Dharma' has a vast variety of meanings, one of which is "duty." But duty in English has the unpleasant connotation of compulsion.* It is something which ought to be done but which, generally speaking, we do not wish to do. Yet in the Buddhist sense it is that which is the next thing to be done, and the emotional labels of dislike or like are not applied. One just does it."*
>
> ***—Christmas Humphreys.***

The work allotted to us has to be performed. The necessity to have to work ceaselessly can enslave us. But we must apply ourselves to work in such a manner that not only does it not enslave us, but actually emancipates us.

Let me but do my work from day to day,
In field or forest, at the desk or loom,
In roaring market-place or tranquil room;
Let me but find it in my heart to say,
When vagrant wishes beckon me astray;
Of all who live, I am the one by whom
"This is my work; my blessing, not my doom;
This work can best be done in the right way."
Then shall I see it not too great, nor small,
To suit my spirit and to prove my powers;
Then shall I cheerful greet the labouring hours
And cheerful turn, when the long shadows fall
At eventide, to play and love and rest,
Because I know for me my work is best.

—Henry Van Dyke.

❑❑

---

* "When a stupid man is doing something he is ashamed of, he always declares that it is his duty!"

—Bernard Shaw in 'Caesar and Cleopatra'

4

WORK, THE EMANCIPATOR—II

"Action rightly renounced brings freedom:
Action rightly performed brings freedom
Both are better
Than mere shunning of action."

—The Bhagavat Gita

EXPECTATION OF RETURN

Elsewhere in this volume, we have touched upon the concept of the present-day world, of each act of ours being taken as a commercial transaction-a sale. In other words, we are all traders selling various things for a profit! Mind you, a merchant cannot continue in business if he gives his wares away except for a price that is higher than what it is intrinsically worth or what it has cost him if he has bought it initially for resale. Suppose that you are the owner of a coal mine. To get coal from the mines, it costs you some definite amount. You just cannot afford to sell coal at that cost or anything less: you are in the business of coal-mining to make a profit. It goes without saying.

Consciously or unconsciously, or by mere force of habit, extending this commercial attitude to all our activities, what has happened? We expect a return for each and everything we do. If we love, we expect to be loved in return. If we help, the man helped by us must repay at least in gratefulness. We are decent and courteous because that is the only way we can expect others to be so towards us. This is a vicious circle—this expectation of return. We become slaves since we are unable to do anything except for a return.

Now, what is the way out? How to break this vicious circle: everybody expecting a profit for everything one does or gives? Is it not a simple solution that we just stop expecting a return? Then it will be a curious commerce indeed! A merchant just giving away his wares without collecting any price, not to say profit!! The miracle: he ceases at once to be a merchant!!! Suppose there are lots of oranges growing in your garden, much more than what you need for yourself and your family. (This does not apply to you if you are an orange-grower by profession). The surplus you just distribute to others—free. Are you a loser thereby? Apparently yes, really not. Suppose everyone keeps for himself only what one needs and distributes the surplus to others free? You might imagine that there will be utter chaos in the world. That is because in a world where every one is a merchant, nobody can think of a free giver. That is the pity of this world!

Well, we are living in a world which has set conventions and if we do not observe them, we will be reckoned crazy and will probably starve. Then shall we not at least restrict this trading to the absolute minimum? What does that mean, you will naturally ask. We are all familiar with the cooperative movement. In a co-operative society or stores, who is buying, who is selling, who is making a profit and where does the profit come from, to whom does it go? All these are done by members. We should develop this attitude of members, you and me. *We* are buying, *we* are selling to ourselves, *we* are making a nominal profit which *we ourselves* share in the end.

THE WAY OUT

Just give this a trial. When you love someone just do not expect to be loved in return. (But the beauty is that you cannot normally stop the other person loving you, yet you must forget it). You just do not worry if the return love is there or not. If you are on a job, think that you are doing something noble as a service to your fellow men, forget you are working for a wage. Take it that God is providing you with the wherewithal to keep you going. In your own mind dissociate your work and your wage. It is only when you link these two that you start arguing with yourself first, and later with your employer, you will also stop idling your time away while at work since you will not have the satisfaction that by doing so you are getting the better of your employer. Idling is a subtle form of cheating one gets wages for which one does not work.

As we have seen, we all have to work, there is no escape. Even just to exist, we have to breathe, eat, sleep and so on. Is anyone paying us for these activities? Why? Because we are doing these things for ourselves and naturally one cannot pay oneself! Here comes the concept of duty. It has to be done for one's own sake and without attaching any label of pleasant or unpleasant. Then why not do it cheerfully and in the best way one can?

We have to remember that each one of us is a part of this world. The world is not something that is apart from us. If we do something for the world, in reality we are doing it for ourselves. Instead of just telling ourselves that we shall do our duty without expecting any return, it is easier to remember that whatever we are doing, it is for ourselves that we do.

One of the best ways to keep the body and mind healthy is to engage oneself in useful productive work. Activity provides exercise, both for the body and for the mind. We forget ourselves and become one with the work when we concentrate on it. There is no time for worry or introspection. If a man thinks all the time only of the return, the quantity and quality of his work will suffer. It is exclusive concentration alone that makes work will satisfactory both in quantity and quality. His skill grows. His usefulness to the society grows. Thus it becomes easier to see our work as a service to the society and the world.

That is the magic of eschewing the expectation of reward or return. It turns one at once into a selfless worker for the good of the world! And do you stand to lose anything thereby? On the contrary, you gain in every respect—bodily, mentally and materially. ❑❑

5

WORK, THE EMANCIPATOR—III

> *"Keep Thou my feet; I do not ask to see*
> *The distant scene, one step enough for me."*
> ***—Cardinal Newman***

THE TWO SETS OF FORCES

As we have already seen, the result or reaction of an act is latent in itself just as the tree is latent in the seed. As we act, the result or reaction is released in stages, sometimes simultaneously, sometimes immediately after and sometimes later. When water is electrolysed, hydrogen and oxygen are released simultaneously. When we eat, our hunger is assuaged as soon as we consume a sufficient quantity. When we sow a seed, it sprouts after a certain number of days.

But the result can be occasionally retarded or even suppressed. That does not go to disprove the law that the result or reaction is latent in the act itself. If a seed is sown, it may just not sprout. It does not mean that the tree is not latent in a seed. Earlier, something might have 'acted' to stop that 'reaction'. The seed might not have been gathered from a ripe fruit. The soil, the climate or other conditions might not have been congenial to the seed in germinating. But these are not evident. We cannot therefore infer that, in some cases, the results do not occur. Two sets of forces are working simultaneously, one *for* and the other, *against*. Since we are not certain which of the two will prevail in the end, the result is also 'not certain.' This may lead us on many occasions to make wrong inferences.

A popular Sanskrit couplet states: "God does not reward a man for his good acts nor does He punish a wrong-doer". The idea is that, as explained, every act brings about its reaction or result. We have also seen that a cause is at once an effect too. Therefore there is no need for God to intervene to bring about any result. This statement should be taken without prejudice to the theory of grace to which we will have occasion to refer later.

Results of actions can broadly be classified as (a) compensation, (b) retribution and (c) reward and punishment. In nature's scheme, there is a compensation for every sacrifice made. A man remains a bachelor. He may miss the love and affection of a wife and children. But the compensation is that he is freed from the responsibilities that devolve on a head of a family. Similarly, a man who marries has some compensation by way of better care and comfort for the sacrifice he makes by sharing his resources with his wife and children. It can roughly be said that *compensation is the dispensation of nature.*

We all strongly believe that an act, good or bad, brings happiness or grief in due course if it has not immediately followed the act. This assumption is quite right, the only snag being that our judgement of what constitutes good or bad acts is often vitiated by self-interest. Anything not to our liking or not in our immediate interest makes us believe that it must be wrong. The concept of 'poetic justice' is also based on this theory of retribution and this expression is more often applied to the effects of bad or wicked deeds, even though it is equally valid in the case of good or noble acts. *Retribution is thus directly linked to the act.*

EVALUATION OF THE RESULTS

Reward and punishment introduce an outside agency in the evolution of the results of a particular act. Therefore the authority to decide whether an act is good or bad also rests in that outside agency. That is the realm of justice and law. Every age, every country, every community or society has its own laws, canons of justice, jurisprudence. In olden days, so called heretics were burnt at the stake. In our present-day world we have traffic laws which were unheard of in olden days. Islam tolerates polygamy whereas most other religions enforce a monogamic standard. The Britishers, during their rule, jailed or executed many Indians. For the British rulers the latter's acts constituted sedition or treason whereas for Indians they were patriotic or heroic deeds. Thus actions to be judged for their results on the basis of so-called justice have to be viewed in a limited sphere.

In the face of these various agencies which seem to be threatening us from all sides with dire consequences for our lapses and forcing us to be vigilant about our actions, we can draw comfort from the fact that for a normal man of average intelligence with determination, it is fairly easy to lead a peaceful and happy life without contravening the laws of any of the above forces. In fact, just as a criminal alone has to fear a policeman who is the friend of the law-abiding citizen, it is only where our acts transgress some established convention or law that we have to worry about evil consequences.

One might wonder about the existence of so many undetected crimes and how evil doers in such cases escape the clutches of the machinery of law and justice. We have already seen the working of retribution in such cases. Non-detection of crime certainly leaves a loop-hole, but the ordinary citizen refrains from breaking laws not merely from fear of punishment on detection. He has a certain built-in mechanism within himself which guides him by telling him extempore what is right and what is wrong from a given stand-point. This is called conscience which has variously been termed as the 'inner voice,' or the 'God within' and so on. Here again, contrary to popular notion, the conscience is not an infallible guide as it is largely the product of our education and upbringing. It is conditioned by our thoughts and ideals and the impact of social conventions and canons of ethics and morality as adapted by the individual's own reasoning.

It is therefore dangerous to place too great a reliance on the correctness of the 'dictates of one's conscience.*

The treatment of the subject of conscience here needs a little elaboration. Let us take an illustration. When Mahatma Gandhi, (whom the late Dr. Haines Holms, the American Christian Minister, declared from his pulpit way back in 1922 as the greatest man in the world), was assassinated in January 1948, humanity was horrified. Yet he was shot dead by a Hindu youth who possibly sincerely believed that his 'conscience dictated' that he should 'remove' a person whom he considered a menace to his religion. He might have been led to believe by *his* conscience that he was doing his duty for his religion or country. Socrates, the oldest of philosophers and one of the wisest men of all times, was sentenced to death by those who probably honestly believed that he was corrupting the youth of his day by indoctrinating them with dangerous ideas! These are mentioned only to demonstrate the fallibility of an individual's conscience.

RESULT IS AUTOMATIC

We have heard a great deal about a 'liberated' soul, a man who even in this very life has become 'perfect'. One of the aspects or attributes of such a man is that he performs his actions without having to weigh each of them and he always does the right or beneficial things. It may puzzle us as to how a man can always be right in his action. This, again, is because we have such funny ideas about life in general. Therefore, let us take a concrete example to drive home the concept of right action—that of a motorist. Who

---

* Conscience itself works in much the same way as an electronic computer. The answers a computer gives are reliable only if correct information has been stored in it before it is given problems to solve. In the same way, if your basic beliefs are sound, conscience becomes a valuable guide in deciding what is normally right and wrong. But if your basic beliefs are not sound, your conscience can be misleading.

—Maxwell Maltz, M.D.
'Unlock your Real Personality'
in Reader's Digest.

is a successful motorist? One who uses his vehicle for his daily travel, without breaking any of the traffic regulations; without hurting himself, his car or others and who maintains it in reasonably good repair most of the time. You will admit that such a motorist is rather the rule than the exception. How does he accomplish this? He does not worry unduly about getting involved in accidents or contravening traffic regulations. He just exercises control *every moment* in a relaxed and enlightened manner over his driving and the rest of the result is automatic.

Similarly, if we concentrate on *this moment* and see that we are engaged in right and beneficial acts as we go through life, all our actions, hours, days and years are automatically watched and safeguarded against pitfalls. *This moment*—it is precious, it is sacred. It is our salvation or our doom. What is stated here should not be taken to mean that there is no need to look ahead. On the contrary, all our actions are geared to reach our goal which will be accomplished without anxiety or worry if we take care of the work right at hand. The secret of the freedom of the liberated soul is this: After a period of watching over 'this moment', perfection becomes a habit, a solid foundation. Sinning is deviating—just a traffic accident in the journey of life. A good motorist is involved in an accident rarely, if at all, and motoring is not a hazardous occupation, to use life-assurance parlance. In the same manner, we too can become accident-proof in our journey through life when we know the aim, the mechanics of living and remain vigilant, concentrate on the work at hand, at the moment.

In the words of William James, the great American psychologist:

> *"Let no one have anxiety about the upshot of his education, whatever its line may be. If he keeps faithfully busy each hour of the working day, he may safely leave the final result to itself."*

And Emerson has said much the same:

"Don't waste life in doubts and fears; spend yourself on the work before you, well assured that the right performance to this hour's duties will be the best preparation for the hours or ages that follow it."

SUMMARY

In the preceding three chapters, we have covered such vast ground that it would be worthwhile summarising here our conclusions or points:

1. We do the work which is at hand. By some strange dispensation (if you delve deep, it will not be so strange!) a particular work is allotted to us and it is to be done by us.
2. Do it to the best of our ability and in the best manner possible.
3. While doing our duty, we should avoid the feeling that we are 'helping' some one. We are doing what we should, without attaching the label of pleasant or unpleasant.
4. Avoid undue attachment to or unnecessary anxiety about the outcome.
5. Do not be indifferent to the action, method or result—only avoid exultation at the prospect of success and depression at the prospect of failure.
6. Do not take credit or blame for success or failure, taking into consideration the fact that there are several agencies which contribute to the so-called success or failure.
7. By constantly being engaged in beneficial and necessary work, we are aware that we not only avoid the pitfalls of being idle, but also develop ourselves for higher assignments which will come to us automatically.
8. By correct application of energy, both physical and mental, we make it go a long way just like the money we earn will go a long way if spent judiciously. Energy, like money, is not just something to be saved or spent. It must be spent on the right thing in the right proportion at the right time.

9. This outlook results in *acceptance* of life with all its bright and dark aspects and not in *resignation.* Acceptance is a positive approach whereas resignation is negative. There is a tinge of despair in resignation while acceptance means according a welcome to a thing irrespective of whether it pleases, or not, at the moment.

10. In summary, the ideas or theses in these chapters represent

    (a) The Philosophy of Work
    (b) The Law of Work and Resultant Action
    (c) The Path of Work As a Means for Liberation.

❑❑

6

A PRESCRIPTION FOR NARROWNESS OF MIND

*"Our own insufficiency is that we live in a fraction of ourselves. In a narrow **I**, in a narrow vision,* in time, *in a belief that the material universe of the moment is all. The perfecting of oneself, the attainment of unity, is connected with.... fulfilling which must mean, to begin with, an overcoming of our narrow temporal vision-so that now we can understand better why the Hermetist advises the exercise of thinking of the life as* living at all points, *in a movement towards 'eternal life.' But time-life-is only one track through the fullness of things."*

—Maurice Nicall

REAL BLESSINGS SELDOM COME EXCEPT IN DISGUISE

It is evening. A young lady is getting ready for a party. She will be meeting a lot of people. Quite a few of them may be her admirers. She is happy anticipating a pleasant evening: nice things to eat and drink, music and dancing, a little progress in her campaign to find a suitable husband. But, look! The next moment she is in agony—she is wringing her hands in despair, she breaks down and sobs. Why? What happened? The sky has suddenly become overcast and it is drizzling outside. The rain is becoming heavy. Her fine dress might get wet. The rain will spoil the party. Very likely it might even be cancelled. She curses the unexpected rain.

Now this girl in cursing the rains is thinking only of her party and her own pleasure. Therefore what is quite a natural phenomenon has become unwelcome. If only she could understand that it is indeed welcome to the farmer, and it is not quite so abnormal to rain in that season, will she weep?

Let us take another case. You have, after a great deal of care and search, bought for yourself a fabulous wrist watch. You are proud of it. You tie it around your wrist and are going about, your head high, and just glancing about, expecting others to notice that you are the possessor of an excellent watch. Your friends, of course, have observed it and are making enquiries about its price etc. Just then an unknown man asks you the time. With great satisfaction, You glance at it and tell him the 'correct time'. But the fellow sneeringly retorts: "Do you call it a watch? The correct time is nowhere near what it indicates. You better throw it down the gutter!" What is your reaction? Won't you feel that he has humiliated you unpardonably? Wouldn't you feel like tearing that fellow to pieces? Yet consider what he was doing in reality. He was just making a remark about an inanimate mechanical contrivance. Suppose the remark had been made in your hearing about the same watch while it was exhibited, before you bought it, in the show-case of a watch-maker? Would you have been the least bothered?

I once seriously fell ill. I became a weakling a poor specimen of a youth of just twenty. I called on a good doctor, who had a reputation for sincerity and skill in his profession. He examined me and when I was expecting him to sympathise with me in my condition, smiling he told me: " You should thank God that you are so ill !" I was puzzled: Thank god that I was ill! Think of it? But he took good care of me and soon the whole picture changed. After that spell of ill-health, I have never had any illness worth mentioning for over two decades. You would be curious (as I was at that time) to know what the doctor meant when he made that seemingly strange statement. Indeed, I asked him a few years later, and surprisingly, he had not forgotten his remark. "Well," he replied. "Real blessings seldom come except in disguise. You had neglected your health, it appeared, for such a long time that you had reached a stage when it compelled you to give it the care it needed." That was, no doubt, true.

Is it not strange how our ego colours external things and distorts their true form? In the aforesaid instances, the unpleasantness of the rain, the bitterness in the criticism of your wrist watch and the sting in the doctor's casual remark, were all caused by one thing: want of detachment. Or to put it another way, lack of proper perspective. That again is due to the narrow thinking we generally are guilty of. To get the right perspective, one has always to think and analyse. We have to delve deeper. Such thinking need not necessarily have to be involved or sophisticated. Often a correct perspective results from simple, straightforward thinking as of a child. In fact a wise man has been compared to a child; a mad man; a drunkard. See what the Bible says:

> *"Unless you be converted, and become as little children, you shall not enter the Kingdom of Heaven. Whosoever therefore shall humble himself as this little child he is the greater in the Kingdom of Heaven."*
>
> ***—Matt. XVIII-3***
>
> *"Whosoever shall not receive the Kingdom of God as a little child shall in no wise enter therein."*
>
> ***—Luke 18:17***

The idea is that wise men are all simple and straightforward in thinking and in looking at things which is in contrast to that of seasoned, wordly-wise grown ups.

> *"Those who would be the Children of God, must take good heed that their words be simple, clear, truthful and guileless."*
>
> ***—St. Francis de Sales***
>
> *"A drunken man who falls out of a cart, though he may suffer, does not die. His bones are the same as other people's; but he meets his accident in a different way. His spirit is in a condition of security. He is not conscious of riding in the cart; neither is*

he conscious of falling out of it. Ideas of life, death, fear and the like cannot penetrate his breast; and so he does not suffer from contact with objective existence. If such security is to be got from wine, how much more is it to be got from God?"

—Chuang Tzu

Is this not true of a tiny tot too?

"Nothing tends so much to produce greatness of mind as methodical, conscientious investigation of the functions of every object; its value in relation to the sum of things and to man as a citizen of that highest state wherein all others are, so to say, families." So wrote Marcus Aurelius in his diary. A discussion of his 'Meditations' follows in one of the coming chapters of this book and no one who has made a serious study of it need look elsewhere for a prescription for healing that all too common malady, narrow-mindedness.

We often accuse ordinary people of narrow-mindedness. Yet even highly educated and cultured people exhibit this weakness in many of their viewpoints. We attach undue importance to certain aspects of life which a little sober reflection will make us laugh at ourselves. When a young man makes a great fuss about his love for a particular girl, the detached onlooker smiles and says as Bernard Shaw said: "How foolish to stake one's happiness differentiating so much one member of the opposite sex from another!" C.E.M. Joad jokingly cautioned our young men: 'Don't' run after a bus and a girl-another will be along in five minutes!" We are only too ready to fall in line with the Joneses. We are conditioned by the opinion of other people, according to which the body is for sensual indulgence, and the world owes us a great deal of pampering. Comfort, ease, cosiness, these are our goals. We take great care and trouble to alter external conditions to bring us a sense of well-being, 'euphoria' as it has come to be known. Yet with a little mental adjustment we can scoff at the power of outward objects or conditions to affect our mental poise, and frequently our bodily well-being.

MAINTAINING A BALANCED OUTLOOK

How many of us consciously care to maintain a balanced outlook, mental equilibrium? Moderation, temperance are strange to most of us. Maybe we are able to achieve moderation in the less important matter of eating and drinking, but when it comes to thinking probably moderation is farthest from our thoughts. We do not at all think or realise that it is necessary. Yet the world or even the universe depends on balance, equilibrium. We methodically vote for an extreme swing of the pendulum. In a prosperous country like the USA is it not strange that the word Communism should raise such scare? There has been a similar phobia for everything "Capitalistic" in the communist countries.

Detachment is what we need. Be an observer, a witness, even to the chatterings of your own mind.

Just stand aside and watch yourself to by
Think of yourself as "he" instead of "I".

— Strickland Gillian, *Watch Yourself Go By*

Remind yourself as Marcus Aurelius did: "Seest thou how few things are needful for man to live a happy, God-like life?!" No one suggests that we should do away with necessities, even luxuries sometimes-whether of the mind or of the body. It is indeed difficult to draw a line between luxuries and necessities. There is a streak of truth in the famous epigram of Oscar Wilde "Give me luxuries, and I shall do away with necessities!"

"Behold, eating, drinking, clothing and other necessities appertaining to the support of the body, are burdensome to a fervent spirit. WIS. IX. 15. Grant that I may use such things with moderation, *and not be entangled with any inordinate affection.. but to require superfluities and such things as are most delightful Thy law forbids; for otherwise the flesh would grow insolent against the spirit-GAL. V. 17. In all this I beseech Thee let Thy hand govern and direct me, that I may in no way exceed."*

— Imitation of Christ

This need for moderation is more applicable to our thoughts. Let us deliberately slow down the process of passing judgement on men, matters or things, even the most insignificant of them. "Let the court suspend all judgement". "Judge not lest yet be judged". Narrowness of mind can vanish only with the dawn of breadth of vision just as the darkness of night will vanish only with the dawn of daylight.

❑❑

7

HAS CHASTITY NO PLACE IN THE MODERN WORLD?

> *"The fact is we are facing an old fight between orgy and self-control, promiscuous living and decent family life, a fight which has been waged again and again across the centuries, upon the outcome of which depends whether we human beings are really going to be human beings or beasts".*
>
> **— *Harry Emerson Fosdick***

BODY—THE TEMPLE OF GOD

It may seem incongruous to touch upon this subject in a book on: "SUCCESS THROUGH POSITIVE THINKING". But its relevance will be clear when we realise that there can be no running away from the fact that this physical body, meant to be the temple of God, calls for and deserves a definite measure of legitimate attention.

> *"Jesus called the body the temple of the Spirit and appears to have led the simple hardy life conducive to optimum health. Yet he also contributed to the gaiety of the wedding feast. His injunction..... certainly indicates that he did not under-estimate the importance of the normal body urges".*
>
> **— Muriel Wrinch, *Key to Living***

When the emphasis is transferred from the temple itself to its occupant, namely God, our life falls into its proper place. As Thomas à Kempis says,

"It is not lawful to cast them all away,
for nature must be supported".

A saint has reached a stage where he need not worry about the temptations of the flesh. But those of the world, aspiring to live the higher life, are confronted with many distractions, not the least of them being the sex urge, variously called the "animal in man", "lust", "carnal desire" and so on. Even a great soul like Gandhi had once confessed that the "animal in him" needed careful watching!

To tackle any problem, we have first to gain a clear understanding of what it actually is. Knowledge alone can save us from the many snares and pitfalls in our path. Therefore let us analyse the implications of leading a chaste or unchaste life from the standpoint of ordinary men and women.

Who can find a virtuous woman? For her price is far above rubies.
— Old Testament, Proverbs xxx, 10

My chastity's the jewel of our house,
Bequeathed down from many ancestors.
— Shakespeare, All's Well That Ends Well, IV, 2

IMPORTANT PART IN THE LIFE OF MAN AND WOMAN

The sex urge in man is often compared to fire. Fire has been harnessed to serve mankind in various ways, and its controlled use has been always necessary and beneficial in man's day-to-day living. Yet every day we hear of fire accidents and conflagrations, causing untold misery, deaths and damage to property. Similarly, sex is the prime urge in man which is the means of perpetuation of the species. Therefore it certainly plays an important part in the life of man and woman, but unbridled licence is more devastating in its effect than fire. The sex urge is fundamentally associated with the maternal instinct. In woman it manifests as the tenderness and self-sacrifice spontaneously forthcoming in a mother for the welfare of the offspring and in men, as a protective emotion towards the weak and helpless.

We also know that the mutual attraction to the sexes, when elevated to a higher plane, is a sublime feeling known as love. It is the starting point in setting up man's primordial invention, the family. Just as a large country, to be governed efficiently is broken up into smaller units like districts or counties, the welfare of humanity needs a smaller, more or less autonomous unit known as the family. Man takes a wife to set up a family as he has, like his wife, till then formed part of a larger one which, when it has grown to a certain size has to be decentralised.

In any consideration of the sex instinct, its association with this concept of the family system is foremost in any civilization. In nature's dispensation, it would be clear that everything is so arranged that all other factors are subordinated to the central idea of maternity. This can be seen even in the bird and animal kingdom.

SUPREME FUNCTION—THE MUTUAL ATTRACTION OF THE SEXES

It is also self-evident that woman is so constructed that she could perform the supreme function of bearing children. The mutual attraction of the sexes, too, is meant to bring them together for the purpose of procreation. But there is no denying the fact that it is not always the conscious urge for procreation that brings man and woman together. Children seem almost the by-product of sexual mating! Here again there need be no wonder since, we have already seen, in nature's scheme, every effort or sacrifice has its compensation and the pleasure, which should be incidental, is a type of compensation to both man and woman for assuming the exacting responsibilities of parenthood.

Nevertheless, it must be admitted that woman's beauty has been played up considerably by poets, artists and mere sensualists. Unquestionably, nature's purpose has been pushed to the background and feminine charm extolled for its own sake and merely as an object or instrument of man's sensual pleasure. In fact, if in man's imagination, the primary attraction of the 'fair sex' has come to occupy a place out of all proportion to its reality, it is because he is a conscious or unconscious victim-and, maybe, not an unwilling one-of conditioning by the poet's ravings over feminine beauty, the novelist's theme in romantic fiction, the artist's glorification of the nude, the beautician's advertisement about the "sex appeal" of a woman's well-groomed, lustrous hair, the flawless "school-girl" complexion etc., and the dress maker's emphasis on the accentuation or the "effective" exhibition of her secondary sex characteristics. In primitive society, woman's sexual role was a private matter whereas in the present-day-world, her "personality" is sought to be built around her physical features, certain types of which have been glorified on the basis of their so-called sex appeal.

It is the considered opinion of men who ought to know that the discovery that conception need not necessarily follow sexual mating has had a profound significance for man not devoid of harmful impact on sexual morality. The function of maternity has been given a place of secondary importance and sex for pleasure has assumed an alarming urgency amounting to an obsession. Modern contraceptive methods have, like nuclear fission, two entirely divergent aspects. One the beneficial and constructive, the other, harmful and destructive. Whilst there is the slogan "Atom for Peace", the horrors of Hiroshima and Nagasaki are still fresh in our minds. Similarly, contraception on the one hand makes for the health of the mother and the offspring by taking away the element of accident and on the other, it promotes sexual licence within and promiscuity outside marriage by making it possible to prevent unwanted or inconvenient pregnancy.

Another sad development in the world today is that woman in various stages of semi-and full nudity is held up in the guise of art as an object of admiration to behold and contemplate and is being fully exploited commercially for many purposes like boosting sales through sexy advertisements and in the motion picture industry. Sexuality has also been subtly linked to the craving in every woman to be attractive for various purposes; to get employment of all sorts, particularly as models and film stars, and above all, for getting a husband.

Thus with her active connivance, man who claims that he has given vast freedom to woman, has made her a willing slave, converting her and her built-up attraction into articles of merchandise. "Sex and sex-appeal for sale and sales" seems to be the slogan! He has hypnotised her into believing that it is for her welfare that he is exploiting her sexually. A generation earlier, women were fully clad, their freedom was "restricted" and their social appearance among males was reduced to a minimum. Then she was held out as a serf! But what is the fact? Is woman any the freer? True, earlier her freedom was deliberately curbed, but then she was not exposed to exploitation by all and sundry-this restriction was meant to be more a protective step for the welfare of both man and woman.

All religious and moral teachings are aimed at reducing temptations where it cannot be done away with altogether. It is plain commonsense that it is always better to eliminate temptations than to expect that there will be sufficient will power available to withstand it. To quote Aldous Huxley. "To temptations of any kind, if repeated often enough, most human beings who are not saints almost inevitably succumb. That is why Christ taught his disciples to pray that they should not be led into temptation. This is, or should be, the guiding principle of all social reform-to organise the economic, political and social relationships between human beings in such a way that there shall be, for any given individual or group within the society, a minimum of temptations to covetousness, pride, cruelty and lust for power. Men and women being what they are, it is only by reducing the number and intensity of temptations that human societies can be, in some measure at least, delivered from evil". In their old, wise ways, our ancestors kept away temptation by placing various restrictions in the way of men and women coming too close to one another, particularly in solitude.

ELEVATION OF CHASTITY

Now, let us come straight to our subject, chastity. There has been a natural elevation of chastity as a virtue both by men and women. Even the most sophisticated among men may not like to marry a girl who is not chaste. While exaggerating the sex appeal of the feminine form, poets have at the same time glorified chastity, and built around virginity an aura of purity, innocence, beauty and nobility. Maybe it is this glorification of the state of virginity that is at the bottom of the idea of the "*Immaculate* Conception of Christ by *Virgin* Mary".

Even medical scientists have recognized the rightful place of chastity in life. Dr. Isabel Emslie Hutton, M.D. says, "If it is only because of the risk of having a child that the modern woman remains pure*, the standard of today is indeed a low one. The great majority of young women undoubtedly remain virginal up to the time of marriage either from high motives and ideals, or the force of family and public opinion". Anything done in contravention of accepted moral principles leads to a feeling of guilt and consequent psychological complications. That is why Freidrich Nietzche says, "There is no happiness in anything we do unless it is the beneficiary of the stamp of approval of the society we live in".

Chastity is founded essentially on self-restraint and self-discipline. Like many other virtues, it is the outward expression of inward discipline. Dr. Gladys M. Cox has beautifully summarised the idea thus: "The girl who has become accustomed to exercise reasonable self-discipline in the ordinary affairs of life is more likely to control her sex life satisfactorily than the one who is, to a large extent, the willing of unwilling victim of her impulses, and has never valued discipline." Havelock Ellis too has described the instinct of chastity in a very striking manner: "Chastity may be better defined as self-control within the sexual sphere....... I once overheard a girl of about fourteen reproaching a companion

---

*A scientist to talk of "purity" in this context! It must have been intuition, because the word chastity is derived from the Latin word *Castus*, meaning pure!!

of about the same age for greediness: "You have never learnt self-restraint!" "It is not necessary", replied the other. " It is not necessary", retorted the first, "it is nice". That girl would, in later life, have no difficulty in understanding chastity. It is the manifestation of temperance, of the *Greek Sophrosyne*, in the sphere of sex. Chastity is a virtue independent of all creeds and religions..... On a purely human basis, chastity has been and still remains a virtue."

Chastity is a virtue only if it is natural and not when it is forced upon woman by others, especially man. To quote Havelock Ellis again: "When chastity is transformed into a mere compulsory continence, it ceases to be either natural, or a virtue, or beneficial. Its essential character is lost sight of." Referring to be extreme restraint, particularly imposed by religion or society on the one hand, and intemperate sexual licence on the other, he says: "These oscillations are the more or less unfortunate exaggeration of a virtue which is still to be cherished. It is not only demanded for the sake of maintaining its human dignity." Beyond that, it is essential to any gracious art of love, which is, as it has been put "the art of touching the things of sex with hands that remember their aptness for all the fine ends of life".

To go back to Dr. Gladys M. Cox, "There is a tendency nowadays to excuse and encourage lack of self-discipline on psychological grounds. Modern psychology is often misrepresented—sometimes with deliberate dishonesty—as providing justification for all kinds of undesirable behaviour. We hear that it is harmful to repress a natural instinct; and that this is particularly so of the powerful sex instinct. The suggestion is that the very act of repression is necessarily injurious. A little reflection will, I think, lead us to see the absurdity of such a contention. We all, in our daily lives, experience all sorts of urges and impulses, some of which are antagonistic to one another, and some of which would lead us into sharp conflicts with our fellows; it would be quite impossible to indulge all of them, however much we wished to do so..... It is of the greatest importance to settle in your own mind whether sexual incontinence is justifiable (before marriage) for, an honest wish to be continent is of considerable help in the struggle ahead."

Conventions are the outcome of the accumulated wisdom and experience of past generations who have learnt their lessons and paid the price for their mistakes. It is indeed pleasantly surprising to hear a member of the medical profession say, as does Dr. Gladys Cox, "There is something furtive and undignified—a "loss of caste"—about an irregular sex relationship and almost without exception a girl comes to regret such illicit affairs".

LOYALTY & DISLOYALTY

It cannot be denied that the question of divorce is closely related to chastity and the monogamic standard.* If chastity is voluntarily accepted as an essential virtue, surely there will be a sharp decline in the number of divorces since a loyal and virtuous wife does not entertain, or allow to take root, any fascination for a man who is not her husband. It is simple common sense that once a woman is determined to be loyal to her legal mate, her entire mental attitude is attuned to that ideal, and thereby she remains steadfast at all times to it. It is the lack of will that is responsible for the liberties we allow ourselves which, step by step, lead to disloyalty of either partner and consequent contemplation of divorce. It is again the needless magnification of a passing fancy which makes a woman waver and which, in turn, encourages a man to take advantage of the situation.

Sexual licence, which often parades in the name of sexual freedom, reduces woman to the level of an instrument of pleasure instead of a dignified human being. For casual sexual encounters outside marriage are hardly the result of mutual respect. As Simone de Beauvoir in her book "The Second Sex", has very penetratingly analysed, for man it is a sort of conquest or triumph and for the woman proof of her "attractiveness." It should not be forgotten that woman

* "I conclude from experience that chastity and monogamy are twins. They stand for the dignity of both the man and the woman".

—Ernest Gordon

has a respected place in society and in the home as mother, as sister and daughter. If her status in these relationships is to receive due recognition, she has to maintain her dignity and chastity and it does not take much thought to understand that her self-respect and her prestige are incompatible with a life of questionable virtue. We rarely come across cases (of course, in the normal way) where a father, a son or a brother, or for that matter, a mother, daughter or a sister of a woman reconciles himself or herself to deviation by her from the ideal of chastity or steadfastness in virtue in sexual matters.

Is chastity coincident with romantic love and love-marriage? As already stated, it is closely associated with monogamy and includes premarital sexual continence. In the form it is practiced in Western countries, especially America, selection of a mate which begins with " dating" is hardly an innocent process as one goes through several "dates" and "crushes" before one settles down to a final choice. In any extra-marital intimacy, it is the feeling of the man and woman concerned towards each other that is uppermost in their minds. Whereas in marriage, the consideration of children and their welfare is what should matter most. As Bertrand Russell in his book, "Marriage and Morals", states: "The view that romantic love is essential to marriage is too anarchic, and like St. Paul's view, though in an opposite sense, it forgets that children are what make marriage important. But for children, there would be no need for any institution concerned with sex, but as soon as children enter in, the husband and wife, if they have any sense of responsibility or any affection for their offspring, are compelled to realise that their feelings towards each other are no longer what is of the most importance." And don't forget that Russell was the first of the iconoclasts who was punished for his unconventional views on marriage, sex and chastity.

The ideal of self-denial is as old as civilization. Any indulgence in sex disregarding religious and moral considerations is, to say the least, a selfish act while all civilized behaviour, even the most insignificant of them, is built around self-abnegation. Though one would not like to go to the extreme by prescribing sexual intercourse exclusively for begetting progeny, there is every reason to believe that it is healthful both for the mind as well as the body, to confine it to relationship within marriage, and that too, in moderation, exercising discrimination. After all, as one writer very aptly put it, "There is nothing outside marriage which could not be done within it!" Within marriage the elements that make for nervous tension, like fear of detection, hurry, incomplete harmony and many other dissonant factors are eliminated. Marriage is like a fortress within the secure walls of which mental health and a clean conscience, let alone physical well-being, can be preserved, liberating man to devote himself to nobler tasks. Thence the sanctity of marriage as a religious and spiritual bond and the emphasis on legitimacy of children whose advent fulfils the natural longing in woman for maternity.

It is not strange or accidental that chastity is propounded as a religious virtue. Religion strives hard to elevate man to the realm of the spirit, subordinating the various hungers of this physical body which tend to drag him down to the abyss of unenlightened selfishness. At the beginning of this chapter, we dwelt on the legitimate attention that is our body's due, but placing undue emphasis on the body's functions, its needs, real as well as imaginary, has several implications which are discussed in another chapter.

INCOMPATIBILITY IN WEDLOCK

By the monogamic standard, divorce resulting in remarriage does violence to the concept of chastity. Remarriage, where it takes place on account of the death of one of the partners may, however be equated to ordinary marriage. Incompatibility in wedlock is a phrase which covers a multitude of sins. If marriage is considered a bond that could easily be got out of—in other words, if the door for easy divorce and remarriage is open—there will be no serious attempt on the part of seemingly incompatible couple to compose their differences, to adjust to each other and make their individual feelings subserve the welfare of the family as a unit and their children, the more important beneficiaries of the family tie. In most cases, it never occurs to the dissatisfied partner or couple, that there can be real reunion of hearts even when there had been a rupture, and divorce is no solution to their problems, inspite of the fact that instances where divorced partners return to each other nostalgically, or remarriages after divorce see the partners none the better for it, are not at all uncommon.

The sex urge often appears to be indiscriminate in its selection of the object of its fulfilment, but in reality such an assumption is not compatible with the orderly existence of human societies. And promiscuity is definitely no answer. Nor would it be right to believe that indulgence would exhaust the urge and extinguish the fire of desire. On the contrary, the more free reins are given to inclination to promiscuous relations, the more the craving for it will grow. It is only by wise self-restraint on the part of both men and women that we can hope to keep unhealthy impulses in check. Every effort at restraint makes practice of future self-control easier. As Shakespeare inimitably put it,

"Refrain tonight;
And that shall lend a kind of easiness
To the next abstinence: the next more easy;
For use almost can change the stamp of nature,
And either curb the devil or throw him out
With wondrous potency......."

—Hamlet

What chastity is to woman continence or wise management of the sex urge is to man. Almost all religions are severe in dealing with adultery. Many of them assert that sublimation* of the sex urge transmutes it into energy and prolongs man's life and confers on him extraordinary mental powers and physical vigour, besides enabling achievement of that undistracted concentration so essential for spiritual life. It is not difficult to understand that there is greater need for watchfulness on the part of man as he is not protected by natural modesty or fear as in the case of woman. His aggressive masculinity (the 'animal in him') can cause untold misery if it is not restrained by the exercise of his intellect, that is, by intelligent self-control, guided by the conventions and laws of society and religion. If, with restrictions staring him in the face at every turn, there is still difficulty for man in keeping his impulses in check, we can very well imagine the anarchy that would prevail if he were to live in a society in which he is free to give unbridled vent to his elemental passions.**

Moreover, it is common knowledge that sexual lapses blunt his finer sensibilities which, in turn, make him impervious to the condemnation of society and religion, thus paving the way for his slow, but sure, degradation. History records that mighty empires and ancient civilizations crumbled once their nationals lost themselves in the morass of immoral indulgences, specially sex, overriding the objections of society or religion.

We began this chapter with a quotation from Dr. Harry Emerson Fosdick. We can do no better than conclude this discussion with another from the same eminent personage, who has spelled out for us the eternal problem thus: "The choice before us is not *whether* our natural impulses shall be restrained and controlled, *but how* it shall be done."

❑❑

---

* "Learn to transmute your sex emotion into the attainment of your definite major purpose, at will, remembering that this is a creative force of unknown, unlimited possibilities." **—Napoleon Hill, "The Ten Commandments of Success" NEW, March 1968.**

** "A youth boiling with hormones will wonder why he should not give full freedom to his sexual desires. If he is unchecked by customs, morals and laws, he may ruin his life before he matures sufficiently to understand that sex is a river of fire that must be banked and cooled by a hundred restraints if it is not to consume in chaos both the individual and the group". **—Will and Ariel Durant in "The Lessons of History".**

8

THE MEANING OF MERIT

"For anything worth having, one must pay the price; and the price is always work, patience, love, self-sacrifice - no paper currency, no promises to pay, but the gold of real service."

— John Burroughs

"Blessings ever wait on virtuous deeds."

— Congreve

PAYING THE PRICE

Jones and James were two friends, both reasonably well off, well educated and well settled in life. Jones was an introvert on principle. He felt that one should be law-abiding at every step and firmly believed that self-help was the best help. Following the famous precept, he was neither a borrower nor a lender at any time. He was a self-made man and therefore did not ever try to set any struggling fellow on his feet. He was reserved and hardly ever giving to joking or seeing the lighter side of things. He lived a comfortable and luxurious life, but always observed most of the Commandments, and was a regular church-goer.

James was just the opposite type. He was a happy-go-lucky sort of man, with the "hail-fellow-well-met" attitude — that is, thoroughly extrovert. He never worried much about principles in the abstract, he was ready both with his purse and body to come to the aid of his fellow. He was rather generous to a fault. His presence anywhere was the signal for light-hearted banter and he even indulged sometimes in ribald, raw jokes, which strictly speaking, would have been of questionable taste. Jones often frowned at his friend's profanity. In the ordinary sense of the word, James was not religious and never made a fuss about church-going or reading the Bible.

You could very well guess the impact of these two men on the people around them—wife and children, friends and relations. While Jones was respected, James was loved.

Then came the Wall Street crash and the recession Among the many fortunes that floundered were those of both James and Jones. They had a difficult time. But friends were forthcoming to help James.* Unsought, people showered sympathy on him. Gifts came pouring in and it was an embarrassing situation for James since he had seldom been at the receiving end. However, it was no small comfort to James to see himself so lionized. In course of time, his fortunes revived and he found his former self again.

But the Crash saw Jones literally crash. The blow was severe from which he could hardly recover. There were few sympathisers and no real helpers. His health steadily declined as there was no silver lining in his dark horizon. He became bed-ridden, despondency gripped his heart and within a year, he died. It was doubtful if anyone outside his very narrow circle ever had a kind word for the dead man. He passed off, "unwept, unhonoured and unsung."

---

*James would have as well been telling himself like Jeremy Taylor (who had lost all—when his house had been plundered, and his family driven out-of-doors, and all his worldly estate had been sequestrated): "I am fallen into the hands of publicans and sequestrators, and they have taken all from me : what now? Let me look about me. They have left me the sun and moon, a loving wife, and many friends to pity me and some to relieve me; and I can still discourse, and, unless I list, they have not taken away my merry countenance and my cheerful spirit, and a good conscience; they have still left me the providence of God, and all the promises of the Gospel, and my religion, and my hopes of heaven, and my charity to them, too; and still I sleep and digest, I eat and drink, I read and meditate...... And he that hath so many causes of joy, and so great, is very much in love with sorrow and peevishness who loves all these pleasures, and chooses to sit down upon his little handful of thorns."

Now, comparing and contrasting the conditions of the two friends when they were down on their luck, how do you explain their different experiences? Is it not obvious that James and Jones got back in their hour of need what they had given in their better days in different ways? James would never have thought of repayment, on the part of any one, of the favours bestowed by him nor return of the kindness he had so liberally been scattering in normal times. Yet, in his adversity, his earlier beneficiaries could not ignore him nor forget the benefits he had conferred on those around him. In the case of Jones, he, who swore by self-help, had the boomerang and found himself desolate. It was too late for him to learn of turn a new page. His "principles" could not bring him any tangible benefits.

It is really interesting to refer in this context to an epitaph in St. George's Church, Doncaster, which is said to run:

"That I spent that I had; that I gave that I have; that I left that I lost."

In the proverbs of Solomon, we read, "He that giveth to the poor, *lendeth* to the Lord" and again in the New Testament, our Saviour tells us that "He shall hereafter regard the clothing of the naked, the feeding of the hungry and the visiting of the imprisoned, as offices done to Himself, and *reward* them accordingly."

Even the ignorant and the illiterate have an inborn sense of the meaning of the word "merit." It is significant that it is derived from the Latin "Mereor," meaning, earn. Acquiring merit implies doing something which brings for the doer worthiness of reward.

Now, as we have seen in another chapter, no action or deed is purely good or entirely bad. "Each action is surrounded by evil as fire by smoke". An act is good or evil according as it begets preponderantly good results or bad consequences. This idea of accumulating merit or demerit (also termed 'sin') is not dissimilar to the accounts that are maintained, say, by banks for their individual clients. Every time you make a deposit or interest accrues, there is a credit entry, and for each withdrawal or charge there is a debit entry. Thus at any given time the balance in your account is your "savings." If your bank allows you an overdraft, you have again a debit balance. The angels, according to the creed of the Mussalmans, are incessantly busy in writing down, whilst standing behind or before a man, his good or bad actions. (see the Koran, Chapter VI, verse 61 and Chapter XIII verse 12).

In our lives we perform both knowingly and unknowingly meritorious deeds as also commit sins. We have elsewhere quoted Emerson as saying : "Every act rewards itself first in our own soul, and then in circumstance. People call the circumstance retribution." We can assume that there is an automatic and continuous recording in our circumstances points for every good and bad action of ours. And it finally or at any given time, a balance is struck, that represents our debit (sin) or credit (merit) balance as the case may be. This concept is as old as civilization and is at the base of the idea of Judgement. In the Book of Job, you here Job crying out "Let me be weighed in an even balance, that God may know mine integrity," and goes on to narrate the meritorious deeds he had performed to the "poor, lowliest and the lost." By integrity he refers to his soundness, solvency, not in wordly goods or money, but in merit in the books of God.

THE BALANCE OF TOTAL GOODNESS

In wordly life, every one strives hard to build up material credit—excess of earning or revenue over expenditure. The more a man has such balance, the richer he is, of course. In the same way, all religions exhort and lead every man to build up for himself a considerable credit balance of merit, not only by acts of kindness but even materially, say by contributing the tithe. When each man, woman or child has a comfortable balance of merit and goes on adding to it, the total of goodness or merit in the family, locality, town, county, country and ultimately the world inhabited by people piles up and reflects in the circumstances. This is not at all a preposterous proposition when viewed in the light of and compared to, the meaning of material or monetary credit.

Therefore, building up, or accumulation of merit is the duty of every one of us, both in the interest of oneself and those of others, say one's kith and kin, countrymen and fellow-citizens of this world. Every kind or good act is an investment in kind as opposed to an investment in money. Just read the utterance of Jesus in this light: "He that giveth to the poor, *lendeth* to the Lord." Why the poor? Because the poor cannot repay.

We have referred to the aggregate of "crdit balance" of the inhabitants of a country. Most religions attribute the prosperity or otherwise of a people to the aggregate of the "balance" of merit being credit or debit. Just look up the meaning of the word "visitation" in your dictionary. It is given as "affliction regarded as or compared to a punishment from God (e.g., pestilence, invasion etc.)". Punishment for what? Good deeds? Is it not self-evident? This idea is not to be brushed aside derisively. Why does a war involve several countries and cause untold misery and suffering, and unimaginable barbarity and brutality are brought into play by way of bombings from the air, denying essential supplies like food by blockades and subjecting prisoners to horrible torture? Amid such wars, even global ones, why do some countries miraculously enjoy the blessings of peace? Due to the policies of Government? Who or what is a Government? Who formulates its policies? Are not the people of a country, even where there is no democracy as such, ultimately the moulders of its destiny? Those of us who are not familiar with the humane characteristics of the people of that "Oasis of Europe," Switzerland, which has remained neutral through two World Wars, would do well to take the trouble of acquainting ourselves with the Swiss ways of life and Government. Then you will know that it is no mere accident that that small country has enjoyed not only enviable peace but abundant prosperity, too. One writer says that the Swiss 'have produced as many great men as any four million humans you could pick.' Further, 'they have produced the greatest of all works of art, a society without poverty, without fixed rancours and without swank.'

Here it would be pertinent to refer to what view a great wartime leader had held about earning and accumulating merit—Winston Churchill, who could have had no claims to being either very religious or philosophical—as given by one of his close associates:

> *"What do we really need to save civilization? Sir Winston long ago told us the main truth! It was only one thing, one simple thing; that some hundreds of millions of men and women should set themselves to do* ***good*** *instead of* ***evil*** *and reap therefrom* ***blessings*** *instead of curses."*

Talking of blessings, in the Book of Job, it is really moving (if it is at the same time amusing to some) to read: "If I have seen any perish for want of clothing, or any poor without covering: if his loins have not blessed me........... then let mine arm etc." Let us ever ponder over the following Biblical assurance:

> *"And let us not be weary in well doing; for in due season we shall reap, if we faint not."*
>
> ***—7-9, St.Paul 6th Chapter, Epistle to the Galatians***

CHARITY BEGINS AT HOME

As a matter of fact, many other things can and do begin at home. Religion, love, compassion, service. Yes, service, meritorious service. There can be no greater blessings for parents than to have their children surround them with loving care and tender service, especially in ill health and old age. Who are better placed and equipped than husband and wife to help and serve each other and also comfort and console in moments of distress and share and double the joys of life? Children expect from us, almost as a matter of right, attention and care which should be elevated to the level of service. Let us reap blessings instead of curses in the place where we spend most of our life - the home. Let us set an example to our children by our personal service. There is real magic in being surrounded by loving service. It you want your kith and kin to wonder if they are not angels themselves or among angels, here is the secret: Loving service.*

Gradually it can expand and extend to others in the community and if possible, to our countrymen and the world. For one ever watchful for avenues to serve, there will always be ample scope and enough opportunities. Extend loving service and you shall not fail to get it. If not now, later. If not here, hereafter. If not in the same coin, at least in coins equally negotiable in the realm of mankind and in the Kingdom of Heaven.

❑❑

---

*Self-love but serves the virtuous to wake,
As the small pebble stirs the peaceful lake;
The centre mov'd, a circle straight succeeds,
Another still, and still another spreads;
Friend, parent, neighbour, first it will embrace;
His country next; and next all human race;
Wide and more wide th' o'er flowings of the mind
Take ev'ry creature in ev'ry kind;
Earth smiles around, with boundless bounty blest,
And Heav'n beholds its image in his breast.

— Alexander Pope 'ON VIRTUE'

9

SEEK YE FIRST.......

"And then thou shalt say that the sufferings of this time are not worthy to be compared with the glory to come which shall be revealed in us".

— Rom. VIII. 18

THE POWER OF POSITIVE THINKING

Dale Carnegie and Dr. Norman Vincent Peale are authors whose works are among the most successful and popular in contemporary non-fiction American literature. Their books are widely read and have run into several editions. Dale Carnegie's books have been published in many countries and translated into several languages of the world. While literary success is common to both, they can be considered to be poles apart and to represent two distinct, though not necessarily contradictory, aspects of life: the secular and the religious.

Writing on how his book ('How to Win Friends and Influence People') came to be written, Carnegie asserts that "no practical, working hand-book on human relations ever existed" before he himself supplied the want by writing it. It is interesting to read what he had to say: "In preparation for this book, I read everything from Dorothy Dix, the divorce-court records, and the *Parents' Magazine,* to Professor Overstreet, Alfred Adler, and William James. In addition to that, I hired a trained research man to spend one-and-a-half years in various libraries reading everything I missed, plowing through erudite tomes on psychology, pouring over hundreds of magazine articles ....". I imagine Dr. Peale would have just smiled if and when he read this account of

Dale Carnegie's. "He need not have wasted a minute's effort", Dr. Peale would probably have said. "Dale Carnegie was searching for light holding a torch in his hand all the time! The 'one and only book' which has existed for centuries, which has been read, preached and followed by generations of men, women and children, ignorant and wise, rich or poor - Dale could surely not have been ignorant of that 'book of books', the Bible." What makes me think so? Writing about his own book, "The Power of Positive Thinking", Dr. Peale declares: "I need not point out that the powerful principles contained herein *are not my invention,* but are given to us by the greatest Teacher who ever lived and who still lives. This book teaches applied Christianity; a simple yet scientific system of practical teachings of successful living that works," In another place. Dr. Peale writes: "Christianity teaches that one basic trait will go far toward getting people to like you." In other words, his idea of How to Win Friends and Influence People is "a sincere, and forthright interest and love for people. Perhaps if you cultivate this basic trait, other traits will naturally develop." All of which amounts to just on Biblical quotation: "Seek ye first the Kingdom of God, and .... all these things shall be added unto you."

The Kingdom of God! Where is it? The Bible gives you the answer. "The Kingdom of God is within you." If it is within us, why should we seek it? America has existed from time immemorial. Yet it came to 'exist' for the "old world" only after Columbus discovered it. Similarly, if we are specially asked to seek first the Kingdom of God, there must be a special reason for it. And that is, we are *not* now doing it. Again, why is it that we do not know that the Kingdom of God is within us? The answer is that we are so much immersed in our cloistered cells that our little lives are, after the fashion of the 'Pharisees and publicans," living a superficial life and neglecting the life of the spirit. Yet even from the point of view of the purely worldly, this superficial life is the one least likely to yield the fruits which we so pathetically yearn for. How is it?

Each one of us nourishes ambitions in our lives. It is quite natural. But what are the methods we adopt for their realisation? It might sound illogical, but a little reflection will show that a direct approach, steps aimed straight at the result, will be the least likely to be successful. Success through such methods is, of course, not ruled out, but surely they are not the best to adopt. Let me illustrate:

A man 'suffering' from obesity goes to his physician. The doctor, a medical man, healing the ills of this physical body (in contra-distinction of the healer of the ills of the soul) examines him and prescribes an elaborate course of exercising and dieting and administers medicines to boot. The patient is all set on the result : reducing weight. He fights with his natural inclinations : inertia in doing physical exercise, with his gluttony in the act of dieting, and his imagination which conjures up the pleasures of the palate - delicious dishes and feasts all the time. He gets anxious that the weight may not, after all, go down so quickly and also feels tired because his body is denied energy-producing foods. His mind hovers between thoughts of success and failure in his weight-reducing campaign. Ultimately, when he tips the scales to his or his doctor's ideas of right weight, he is always haunted by the fear that, in the end, it may be only temporary. It also need not cause surprise if, after all the exercising and dieting, the loss in weight had been the result merely of his worries in this connection! That brings to mind the story of the doctor who pronounced 'the death sentence' on his over-weight patient in the hope that the depression thus caused would prove to be just the corrective the sufferer needed!!

Next, let us take a variation to the above imaginary case- nistory. A good citizen is rather over-weight, but not over-religious. A minister in the locality takes a brotherly interest in him. He gives him a personal sermon and extols the virtue of regular church-going, fasting as a religious duty, praying as a means of purifying the mind and so on. The priest induces him, by steps, to visit daily a church situated on the top of a nearby hillock, to pray in silence, to read the Bible regularly, to share his victuals with the poor and also to pray for others' welfare. The man takes to the new path. Gradually, by the exercise of climbing the hill to visit the church daily by reducing the intake of food on religious grounds and without ever brooding over his bodily condition, his weight goes down! Not only does his physical proportions touch normal levels, but, as a bonus, he feels cheerful and mentally alert and consequently his personality itself improves considerably. He becomes a happy, relaxed man, physically fit, mentally joyful with the added satisfaction of feeling that he has acquired religious merit.

THE TWO PATHS

Which of the two paths appeals to you? The result is same in both cases. Yet in one the approach was direct and in the other, the aim was all but forgotten, nevertheless achieved in a more pleasant and durable way. This is true of every sphere of human activity. In a wide sense, it is an incontrovertible fact that what you want has almost always to come as a by-product. Health, wealth, happiness, peace of mind, romantic love, position, fame, prestige, all these are best not pursued exclusively. It is in this context that the declaration of the Bible, "Seek ye first the Kingdom of god" becomes a meaningful postulate. "The joy to be extracted from living is to live for a purpose that is greater than one's own immediate interest," wrote the shrewd, worldly-wise Bernard Shaw. Dr. Harry Emerson Fosdick has said: "Another factor in the pattern of a healthy life is unselfish devotion to persons and causes *outside oneself.*" According to modern psychologists, the factor of utmost importance for mental health is to have a high ideal by which to be guided in day-to-day life. This provides the greatest joy and solace, enabling one to withstand any number of what are ordinarily known as trials. It is common knowledge that in this world the many acts of glory are those that are performed by men and women for upholding certain ideals, certain lofty principles. They remain bright in the history of man, because, in the light of that ideal, the ordinary individual not only forsook with joy the comforts of life, but sometimes even courted death. In the course of such pursuit of ideals, common men and women are often transformed into heroes, saints and savants. Pursue something noble, something unselfish, something really great. Acquire virtue and skill. Keep yourself fit physically and alert mentally. Avoid dissipation and extravagance of all sorts. Then see what happens!

The Kingdom of God is within you! Let us look at another Biblical statement : "For what shall it profit a man if he gains the whole world, and loses his own soul?" (Mark 8:36). These quotations are links in a chain. 'Seek ye first the Kingdom of God which is within you because it does not profit if a man gains the whole world and loses his own soul.' There is a clear distinction between the world outside and the Kingdom of God within you. As mentioned earlier, man's pre-occupation with his physical body and the material world outside is the real hindrance in perceiving the Kingdom of God within. Man perceives himself to be the body and seldom sees himself as the soul. This earthly vessel, this flesh-pot (to use the words of Marcus Aurelius) and this earthly world seem to be incompatible with Man, the Soul, only so long as he is wallowing in the mire of life in the flesh. On the other hand, if you seek the Kingdom of God *first*, you perceive the life in the flesh in its proper perspective.

Here again, let us take an illustration. A boy is learning to ride a bicycle. He first tries balancing, all the time conscious of balance alone - balancing his body and the bicycle. His attention is exclusively given to the cycle and his body. He is afraid that he will fall down or dash against someone or another vehicle might dash against his. He is not able to look ahead, nor remember or recall anything else. But once he has mastered the technique of balancing and riding on bicycle, he can take his mind off the vehicle and balancing (which becomes automatic) and look at the road ahead, cast his eyes around to take in the beauty of the scene, do even serious thinking, sing a song and what not! Can a learner ever think of taking another person on the back seat? Even that becomes possible once he has learnt riding. While learning he practiced in a sequestered spot, but no he plies even in the busiest thoroughfare without fear!

Similarly, once you have learnt to live the life of the soul, you are able to lift the mind above matter, which then loses its all-important aspect and falls in the proper place in the scheme of the universe. For the life in the flesh, everything appears as good or bad only in relation to the pleasures of the physical body, whereas, for the life of the spirit, nothing is good or bad in itself, but everything fits into the universal life.

ASPIRANT AFTER SOUL LIFE

For the life of the soul, the first steps are character-building through prayer, contemplation, meditation and discernment and development of divine qualities. I think it would not be out of place here to give you a glimpse of the requisites of an 'aspirant after soul-life' as given in India's ancient literature.

There are eight essential qualifications for a real aspirant. They are :

1. **Calmness** : *Resting of the mind* steadfastly on its Goal (God) after having detached it from manifold sense-objects, by continually observing their limitations.
2. **Self-Control** : Not allowing the mind to externalise.
3. **Forbearance** : Bearing afflictions without thinking of remedy, with an unruffled feeling (Holy indifference).
4. **Distaste** : Distaste for sense-pleasures.
5. **Faith** : Firm belief in the truth of the scriptures.
6. **Self-settledness** : Constant concentration of the *intellect* on God.
7. **Intense longing** : A burning desire to be freed from the limitations of the life in the flesh and to be established firmly in the Kingdom of God. In other words, in oriental language, intense longing to be liberated.

8. **Discrimination** : Discrimination between the real and the illusory, between the eternal and the transitory, in a continuous process.

It is not to be wondered at if these ideas appear to be somewhat obscure. It can all be summed up in a single phrase: "Dying to self", or enlightened abjuration of selfish thinking, selfish speech and selfish action.

We often hear of divine and devilish qualities. The divine qualities relate to the soul life and the devilish ones to the life in the flesh.

The strange phenomenon of everything good chasing a man who renounces, and eluding the grasp of the man who is chasing them, is all too common in daily life. Thus success in living the higher life of the soul is automatically accompanied by success in temporal life. Since a truly enlightened man does not value worldly success except as a means to further the weal of mankind, he does not crave for it. When it comes to him unsought, he does not shirk his responsibility. Praise and blame do not affect him since he feels he is only the instrument of His will and his motto is "Thy will be done." Failures are not his, either, because of his establishment in the feeling of "instrumentality." He seldom goes wrong as he is quite clear about the objectives, the ends and means are pure because the ends are unsullied by thoughts of personal gain.*

That is why Plato envisaged a Philosopher-King for his Utopia, for his Republic. A Philosopher (not the mere

---

* Read this portrait of the 'Magnanimous Man' which Aristotle drew: "The magnanimous man will behave with moderation under both good fortune and bad. He will know how to be exalted and how to be abased. He will neither be delighted with success nor grieved by failure. He will neither shun danger nor seek it, for there are few things which he cares for. He is reticent and somewhat slow of speech, but he speaks his mind openly and boldly when occasion calls for it. He is not apt to admire, for nothing is great to him. He overlooks injuries. He is not given to talk about himself or about others, for he does not care that he himself should be praised, or that other people should be blamed. He does not cry out about trifles, and craves help from none."

academic, speculating type) is a God-wise man who has no axe to grind. He is cool-headed, clear-thinking and pure-acting because the well from which his life springs is pure, stems from the divine ground. There is no reason to believe that this picture is not true to life. Every age has produced its famous saints. There had also been numerous unknown or obscure saints who demonstrated the truths of different aspects of the divine life inconspicuously in their simple lives.

If we are unable to think of anything sweeter than the life in the flesh, it is because we have never tasted the nectarous sweetness of the higher life. A beautiful Sanskrit couplet calculated to silence the distrust of those who lack experience reads :

> *"A bride who does not know the happiness in store in her husband's house, weeps when she is being taken there. But she refuses to return to her mother's home after she tastes the happiness of marital life."*

The mother's home here is living after the world's ways, and married life is that life which is wedded to God. The same idea is very sensitively delineated in 'My Imitation of Christ' as follows:

> *"But alas! the pleasure of sin prevails over the worldly soul and under these briers she imagines there are delights - Job XXX. 7; because she has neither seen nor tasted the sweetness of God, nor the internal pleasure or virtue."*
>
> ***—Book III Chapter 20***

THE REAL HAPPINESS

We can progress through life only by means of sacrifice. We have to give up (involuntarily, though) infancy and childhood to grow up into adolescence and youth. Even for material security, we have to sacrifice the pleasure of spending today everything we earn, to put away something for a rainy day. If we want to taste the more refined enjoyment of noble thoughts and nobler life, we have to stop indulging in superficial activities which are more transient and transitory. "No man can serve two masters." You cannot eat your cake and at the same time have it. *Real happiness* is vouchsafed only for that brave aspirant who sets at nought the comforts and consolations of the temporal life of worldly people for the greater delights that await him in the Kingdom of God.

> *"Lay not up for yourselves treasures upon earth, where moth and rust doth corrupt, and where thieves break through and steal. But lay up for yourselves treasures in heaven, where neither moth nor rust doth corrupt, and where thieves do not break through nor steal. FOR WHERE YOUR TREASURE IS, THERE WILL YOUR HEART BE ALSO."*
>
> ***—Matt. 6–19-21***

❑❑

10

MEDITATION AND PRAYER—I

"Meditation governs the affections, directs our actions, corrects excesses, softens the manners, adorns and regulates the life, and lastly bestows the knowledge of things divine and human alike."

— Bernard of Clairvaux

"It is easy in the world to live after the world's opinion; it is easy in solitude to live after one's own opinion; but the great man is he who in the midst of the crowd keeps with perfect sweetness the independence of solitude."

— Emerson

"How still, how happy! Now I feel
Where silence dwells is sweeter far
Than laughing mirth's most joyous swell
However pure its raptures are."

— Emily Bronte

THE GREAT PROMISE

The realization at last that religion is antagonistic neither to science nor secular existence has dawned on thinking people all the world over. Many of its theories can stand the test of science. Day by day more and more people realize that religious practices make our secular life more efficient and healthy. It equips us better to deal with the various difficult situations arising even in business and commerce. Indeed the dawn of this realization holds great promise. No one, we can assume, is entirely irreligious. Even those who protest that they believe neither in God nor prayer or meditation can stand out for long because they instinctively feel their inadequacy to face crisis by themselves and unconsciously appeal to a power, which rules the universe, to come to their rescue. Many a saint has begun life as a rough unbeliever, believing only in the power of money to get whatever we want and unaware of any pleasure superior to those of his senses. Most of them were turned to saints at a particular moment in their lives when their eyes were opened by a powerful shock administered to their earlier convictions by some unforeseen incident.

Prayer and meditation, in their highest from, are no doubt the means to establish our identity with the Universal Spirit. But even in less refined forms they have vast blessings to confer on ordinary men and women. As we gain more insight into the verities of existence, through these media, our physical body and mind and intellect derive benefit. Dr. Norman Vincent Peale has very clearly expressed this idea in his dynamic book, *The Power of Positive Thinking*. "It is significant," he says, "that the word "holiness" derives from a word meaning "wholeness" and the word "meditation", usually used in a religious sense, closely resembles the root meaning of the word "medication." The affinity of the two words is startlingly evident when we realize that sincere and practical mediation upon God and his truth acts as a medication for the soul and body." Let us see how.

It is an irony of worldly life that market-place behaviour come into every day transactions - not only those which are purely commercial, but even other activities. Some famous American writers have openly declared their conception of every activity in life as a selling transaction. The use of the word 'selling' is significant. Basically every sale is effected for a profit. When you love, when you marry, when you move in society and even when you give a present to your own wife and children, you are supposed to be selling something at a price higher than its intrinsic worth. Suppose, in the typical American fashion, you bring a box of candy and flowers to your wife. It is a gift no doubt given out of love, but it is certainly not without expectation of return! You expect to make her happy as she is probably receiving what she did not expect. That happiness, in turn, is to be made use of for some selfish purpose. You wish to silence a cantankerous or nagging mate, or you expect the present to influence her behaviour towards you to bring an extra measure of pleasure to yourself.

THE INNER SANCTUARY

But there has necessarily to be a respite from commerce. You just cannot reduce every moment of your life to the level of a purely commercial existence. You need rest, you need peace. Sound and speed, are the twin curses of the jet age. Sound, especially of the sharp, crashing type, has a very deleterious effect on our nervous system. It has also been proved that speed sends up the blood pressure of the driver. Travellers in jet planes are said to suffer from a very shattering fatigue after a journey. It is our every day experience that our thinking process is paralysed by deafening sounds. Read what Christopher Morley writes about 'Mental Erosion Next':

> *"Every human being is endowed with a limited and infinitely precious stock of attention power; and life today is such that—unless the individual is singularly obstinate and cunning—this power of the mind may easily be dissipated or conventionalized by endless competitive demands. By newspapers, by electric lights, by telephone, by radio, by moving pictures, by aeroplane and motor car and church and school and state, by a thousand appeals, admonitions and interruptions, the mind is assailed and distracted. We hear a good deal about the agricultural problem of soil erosion : hill sides denuded of fertile top soil by the actions of streams or great regions of rich wheat lands scoured off by dust storms. Surely not less serious is the matter of* **mind erosion**: *the dust storms of daily excitement and of continual triviality can easily blow away the sensitive top soil of the spirit."*

Therefore it is evident that we need tranquillity, peace. If your own home is a refuge for you from the real market place, there has to be yet another refuge from the market place that is your own home. Where and what can be that refuge? It is the inner sanctuary of your own heart and soul.

When from our better selves we have too long
Been parted by the hurrying world, and droop,
Sick of its business, of its pleasures tired,
How gracious, how benign, is solitude!

—Wordsworth.

You can take recourse to that retreat and regain your poise. You can create for yourself a cell of peace, a haven of joy, a hothouse for spiritual growth. The Emperor of Rome, Marcus Aurelius, in his "Meditation" enjoins himself thus: "Live in thy palace as thou wouldst on a mountain. Let nothing bedim the conviction that in a man's own breast lies the real country retreat and that there is all the peace that can be found on mountain tops, by the sea-side and so forth."

The first step is to withdraw yourself from the world around you as a tortoise contracts its limbs into its shell in the presence of any threat. It is essential that you should seek solitude in a place devoid of disturbance of any sort. The second step is to withdraw the outgoing senses and hold them in check. Then sitting in a comfortable posture - the ideal thing would be to sit on the floor with your legs crossed and folded. You might find it difficult, but practice will make it possible. Then relax yourself completely. Just think that you have hung the coat that is your body on the coat-hanger of your shoulder blades and vertebral column. Deliberately drop tension from each limb, starting from your eyes and face. Close your eyes lightly. If you tighten the eye-lids, darkness envelopes whereas if you keep your eyes half-shut and look at the tip of your nose, there will be an effulgence in the space between your eyebrows.

To facilitate creation of the proper atmosphere, you can use various aids. You can have before you an inspiring picture of your favourite deity. Pictures of natural landscape capturing scenic beauty, a soft light, light incence, these can be used with advantage. When you enjoy peace in this atmosphere, that very atmosphere will later induce the peace and joy for you. You can softly hum a hymn or play a record of a devotional song.

Now, stopping all activities other than breathing, take a few deep breaths. The next thing to do is to stop thinking. This will be a real task. The mind is not so easily silenced. You can address a few words to your own mind : "Calm down, be tranquill" while you relax. If it appeals to you, chant the sound OM which is the symbol of the Impersonal Godhead. Here again, once you associate certain words with the process of relaxation and silencing your mind, in due course, mere utterance of these words or sounds will be attendant with similar result.

A ZERO MENTALLY

While thus becoming a zero mentally, you will also feel as if you have no body—physically you become zero too. You are merely consciousness. Now drink deep this peace, this tranquillity, this negation of body, mind and intellect and assertion of the soul. You will feel free, completely free. By daily practice, one must lift this state higher and higher and associate it with unconditioned, pure joy. This condition has sometimes been termed "the silence" because silence is the essential element in meditation. It is stilling the body, mind and intellect. Thomas Carlyle has said: "Silence is the element in which great things fashion themselves."

"In *sacred* silence of the mind
My heaven and there my God I find."

Why should one "still" all the functions of the body and mind? Here is the answer :

> *"If you wish to tranquillise your mind and restore its original purity, you must proceed as you would do if you were purifying a jar of muddy water. You first let it stand, until the sediment settles at the bottom, when the water will become clear, which corresponds to the state of the mind before*

it was troubled by defiling passions. Then you carefully strain off the pure water ..... When the mind becomes tranquillised and concentrated into perfect unity, then all things will be seen, not in their separateness, but in their unity, wherein there is no place for the passions to enter, and which is in full conformity with the mysterious and indescribable purity of Nirvana."

— Surangama Sutra

"There are three kinds of Silence; the first is of Words, the second of Desires and the third of Thoughts. The first is perfect, the second more perfect and the third most perfect. By not speaking, not desiring, and not thinking, one arrives at the true and perfect Mystical Silence, wherein God speaks with the Soul, communicates Himself to it, and in the Abyss of its own Depth, teaches it the most perfect and exalted Wisdom."

— Michael de Molinos in The *Spiritual Guide*

That the method and process of meditation* herein given are not something revolutionary can be seen if you read the chapter, "A Peaceful Mind Generates Power" in Dr. Peale's book. Indeed he has every reason to regret as he does that "this generation of Americans has missed something that our forefathers knew and which helped to condition their character."

We have already referred to the therapeutic effect of meditation. Starr Daily (as quoted by Dr. Peale) says, No man or woman of my acquaintance who knows how to practice silence and does it has ever been sick to my knowledge." The Noble Prize Winner, Dr. Alexis Carrel, put it more plainly thus: "Those who keep the peace of their inner selves in the midst of the tumult of the modern city are immune from nervous diseases."

When dealing with a topic which is not quite easily comprehensible, we must perforce borrow the description

---

*See appendix *C*

of those who have expressed themselves more intelligibly. Appendix *A* and *B* will give a better idea of 'samadhi' which approximates the state of "super-consciousness."

It is relevant to reproduce here what Joseph Addison wrote early in the eighteenth century as it applies equally, or even more, to the present day:

> *"There are, indeed, but very few who know how to be idle and innocent, or have a relish of any pleasures that are not criminal; every diversion they take is at the expense of some one virtue or another, and their every step out of business is into vice or folly. A man should endeavour, therefore, to make the sphere of his innocent pleasures as wide as possible, that he may retire into them with safety, and find in them such a satisfaction as a wise man would not blush to take. Of this nature are those of the imagination, which do not require such a bent of thought as is necessary to our more serious employments, nor, at the same time, suffer the mind to sink into that negligence and remissness, which are apt to accompany our more sensual delights, but, like a gentle exercise to the faculties, awaken them from sloth and idleness, without putting them upon any labour or difficulty".*

As a variation to the pleasures of imagination held out by Addison, may I recommend to you a daily dose of meditation? Trial costs nothing, and the benefits to be gained therefrom are by no means small. As Michelangelo said: "Recollect that trifles make perfection and that perfection is not trifle." There is no specific dose for the administration of this wonderful medicine. You will find great benefits accruing by practising more often. Regularity is of the utmost importance and as far as possible a regular time should be followed, preferably the early hours of the morn when there is perfect quiet, the air is fresh and cool and the day-break spreads a magical charm on the eastern horizon.

❑❑

11

MEDITATION AND PRAYER - II

"True prayer is a way of life; the truest life is literally a way of prayer."

— Alexis Carrel

PRAYER—A NOBLE PETITION

Prayer is a logical adjunct of the practice of meditation. The great drawback of routine prayer is that is becomes an automatic mental or verbal repetitionery process which frees the mind to roam about in other fields. As Shakespeare wrote:

"My words fly up, my thoughts remain below;
Words without thoughts never to heaven go."

Another poet, too, has echoed the same idea thus :

"In prayer the lips ne'er act the winning part
Without the sweet concurrence of the heart."

— Herrick, *The Heart*

'Words without thought' is the mere verbal repetition of prayer in which the mind does not participate - just empty words. Only consciously uttered prayer, conscious of the purpose, aware of the content and context, can be beneficial and uplifting. This subject of prayer has been discussed threadbare by a variety of writers, poets, preachers, teachers, philosophers and scientists. With the assumed incompatibility of science and religion, it is delightfully surprising that one of the most beautiful treatises on prayer has been written by a world-renowned scientist, Dr. Alexis Carrel, which has been reproduced in Appendix D.

Aldous Huxley in his famous book "The Perennial Philosophy" classifies prayer into four different categories :

a. Petition
b. Intercession
c. Adoration
d. Contemplation.

Petitionery prayer can be lofty and 'unselfish' or childish and beggarly. If you beg of God to show Himself or His wisdom, it is a noble petition. The famous piece attributed to St. Francis of Assissi is the best example of a lofty petitionery prayer :

> *"Lord, make me an instrument of thy peace. Where there is hatred, let me sow love; where there is doubt, faith; where there is despair, hope; where there is darkness, light; and where there is sadness, joy.*
>
> *"O Divine Master, grant that I do not seek so much to be consoled as to console, to be understood as to understand, to be loved as to love; for it is in giving that we receive; it is in pardoning that we are pardoned, and it is in dying that we are born to everlasting life."*

On the other hand, if you ask for worldly prosperity, prayer degenerates into plain begging. As George Bernard Shaw has said, "common people do not pray; they only beg." It is also a fact that few among mortals can ask for fulfilment of any worldly desire that, if granted, would do them undiluted good. What we think are blessings, oftener turn out to be curses.

> *"We ignorant of ourselves,*
> *Beg often our own harm, which the wise powers*
> *Deny us for our good; so find we profit*
> *By losing our prayers."*
>
> **— Shakespeare, *Antony & Cleopatra***

In intercession, the petition is on behalf of others and therefore it is on a definitely higher plane than petition on one's own behalf. Intercessionery prayer can lead to a broadening of fellow-feeling as, if genuine, it springs from real compassion for others. It must be backed by action aimed at relieving others of their suffering when it is possible and involve self-sacrifice.

Adoration which has been described as "the use of intellect, feeling, will and imagination in making acts of devotion directed towards God in his personal aspect or as incarnated in human form." It is distinctly superior to the first two forms, petition and intercession, as it consists in extolling the greatness of God, His glory, His compassion and so on. The Bible shows us the way of prayer belonging to this category:

> *"Our Father which art in Heaven! Hallowed be Thy name. Thy will be done on earth, as it is in Heaven."*

When we conceive of God as anthropomorphic, we delight in describing His glorious form and different aspects of manifestation of His benevolent rule of the universe. While engaged in adoration, we often forget ourselves and our heart and mind merge in Him.

Then probably the noblest and highest form of prayer is contemplation. Aldous Huxley defines contemplation thus: "It is that condition of alert passivity in which the soul lays itself open to the diving ground within and without, the immanent and transcendent Godhead."

Prayer in the from of contemplation is, again, not quite different from meditation. Writing of "Scientific Prayer," Mr. Charles R. Fillmore, Executive Vice President of Unity School of Christianity, says:

> *"Prayer in its purest from is simple. It is a matter of concentrating one's entire intellect on God, affirming a positive statement of truth, meditating on divine principle, and finally turning within one's own being in a wonderful time of quiet called 'the Silence' wherein man becomes receptive to the 'still small voice' of God."*

Indeed, it is extremely difficult to draw a line between these various acts of meditation, petition, intercession, adoration or contemplation. As long as self-consciousness (consciousness of the lower self) is kept in abeyance and the humble human heart goes out in pious, fervent, intensive devotion towards that Power, the One without a second, one will have no need to identify or remember these various names of seemingly different activities.

FLAVOUR OF GENUINE PRAYER

Those who have tasted the rich flavour of genuine prayer will be found to have become enthusiastic prayer-addicts. Oriental saints have in their wise ways stated that the Name (of God) is greater than God Himself. Does God exist in two separate entities? The idea is that to think of God, one has to remember the name, God.

"In the beginning was the Word, and the
Word was with God and the Word was God."

— Gospel according to St. John

Moreover, since we cannot grasp Him easily in His immanent and transcendent aspect, it is we who have need for His Name and Form, or need a Name and Form for Him.

Here is a sweet, simple and sensible exposition of the role of prayer in our lives:

"Be not afraid to pray - to pray is right.
Pray, if thou canst, with hope; but ever pray,
Though hope be weak, or sick with long delay;
Pray in the darkness, if there be no light.
Far is the time remote from human sight,
When war and discord on the earth shall cease;
Yet every prayer for universal peace
Avails the blessed time to expedite.
Whate'er is good to wish, ask that of Heaven,
Though it be what thou canst not hope to see;
Pray to be perfect, though material leaven
Forbid the spirit so on earth to be:
But if for any wish thou darest not pray,
Then pray to God to cast that wish away."

— Hartley Coleridge

❑❑

12

REFLECTIONS ON PERENNIAL PHILOSOPHY

"For I will make thee forget thy pains and enjoy internal rest.

I will lay open before thee the pleasant fields of the Scriptures, that thy heart being enlarged thou mayest begin to run in the way of My Commandments."

— Ps. C XVIII. 32

ATHEISM IS A BLIND ALLEY

There are many religions in this world. Each has sub-divisions or creeds and its own cosmology, theology and philosophy. Yet in the seeming diversity, there is a real unity. There are certain fundamentals common to all, which can be termed the "Perennial Philosophy", which Aldous Huxley has described as the "Highest Common Factor". Belief in God is the substratum of most religions. Certain atheistic strains are not uncommon in some of the creeds. Science, which believes in proving everything, may not agree with many of the theories which religions propound. But atheism is a blind alley and leads us nowhere. To quote the words of Dr. Henry C. Link. "Agnosticism is an intellectual disease, and faith in fallacies is better than no faith at all." There is the famous story of a learned professor who was lecturing to an audience on evolution. He started by saying that at the beginning of time, there was nothing but water, water everywhere. But before he could proceed further, an apparently unsophisticated member of the audience stammered a question: "B-but whe-where did all the water come f-from, sir?" Everyone burst into laughter and the lecturer turned crimson and was non-plussed for a time. The moral of the story is obvious!

We have all heard of Marcus Aurelius. He was Emperor of Rome and follower of the school of philosophy founded by Zeno known as Stoicism. Since Stoicism is not considered as a religion as such, Marcus Aurelius was a "Pagan." Yet history tells us that he was strongly attracted towards the ideals of Christianity. His famous "Meditations" which is in the manner of random reflections on life, temporal, religious and spiritual, has been quoted approvingly and appreciatively by writers of all denominations.

True, Marcus Aurelius did not propound any new doctrine nor did he owe open allegiance to the religious beliefs of his time. Yet instead of that being a drawback, it has been the secret of the great success and popularity of his 'Meditations' which remains fresh even after the passage of nearly 2000 years. Therefore this classic can legitimately be considered reflections on 'Perennial Philosophy.' As one publisher writes: "You will be struck by resemblances to your own era as you read the wise Meditations of the great emperor-philosopher, Aurelius." It is truly remarkable how people of different religious persuasions claim similarities in the 'Meditations' to their own beliefs, ethics, morality and philosophy. This is especially so when we consider how we are all conditioned by the religious thoughts of our own particular sect or creed and find great difficulty in understanding and appreciating the truths as propounded by leaders of other religions. For example, even the most progressive Christian finds it difficult to question the Biblical version of creation. He will also not question the premise that there can be no salvation except through Christ.

THE STRIKING RESEMBLANCE OF HINDU THOUGHT

Plato's dream of a philosopher-king for his Utopia 'Republic' has its parallel in the history of India. There were great emperors who were also great philosophers in ancient India. Therefore it is no wonder that to the Indian mind, Marcus

Aurelius brings recollections of her own 'Rajarshis' (literally, royal saints) like Janaka and Ashoka.

Similarly, Aurelius is very near to Hindu scriptural ideas and conceptions when he avers: "There is only one Universal Substance though it be broken up into a myriad bodies, each with its peculiar qualities. There is but one Soul though the natures and limits of the individuals among which it appears to be distributed are legion. And there is but one Intellective Soul, though it seems divided." The Bhagavat Gita says, "To work alone art thou entitled and not to its fruit" and it is echoed in the 'Meditations': "Deem the action itself reward enough." Luckily for the future welfare of this strife-torn world, more and more people have begun to stress on the points of agreement, rather than harp on differences, among the world religions. I was pleasantly surprised to read a number of articles in the Christian magazines "New" and "Unity" which bore striking resemblance to the central ideas of Hindu thought which find an echo in the passage quoted above.

The following interpretation of Perennial Philosophy against the background of the 'Meditations' certainly deserves examination and study. Let us see how the Roman Emperor viewed life as it is, by what methods he arrives at the futility of mere secular existence, what his idea of the ideal life is, and also the paths indicated by him to reach that goal.

As we know, from the atom to the star, every particle in this universe rings with egotism and it is this that makes what is called the world. This separateness, this idea of 'I' and 'mine' is the main factor which animates the world. While the lower forms of life or consciousness possess this egotism instinctively in common with human beings, it is the sole privilege of man that he can consciously sink his egotism in pursuit of a higher goal. Selfishness limits our vision, separates us one from another and is the cause of all conflict. It we transcend this limitation and viewing ourselves in the proper perspective in relation to the universe and nature, play our part as God intended us, the world would be transformed into paradise.

Strangely enough, his physical body is the first and greatest obstacle to man in his way to a higher life and the main prop for the egotism. He has mistaken his body to be himself and forgotten his soul. With this delusion, he puts his body's requirements above everything else. He decks it with fine dress and ornaments and pampers it with all sorts of indulgences. Any bodily injury or inconvenience becomes grievous to him. He dreads death, shrinks from pain and discomfort and woos sensual pleasure. Thus he develops attachment for, and identifies himself with, his possessions, wife and children - all of which appear to him necessary for his comfort and pleasure. Hence their well or ill being becomes his own. Thus starts a vicious circle termed in Hindu terminology as 'Samsara' (worldly existence).

Secondly, there is another delusion springing from egotism. Man, seeking happiness, confuses it with pleasure and another vicious circle is formed. As we have discussed in an earlier chapter, he goes hunting for pleasures, agreeable sensations, for which he needs objects of their delight. The senses ask for more and out to satisfy them, he becomes their slave. In consequence, he falls a prey to a variety of undesirable emotions like greed, jealousy, fear and anger.

Marcus Aurelius attacks these delusions in diverse ways. First he warns: "In the conception of man, never include this outer vessel, i.e., the body." He dissects the human body and discards it as a filthy, fleshy prison of the Soul, which Death will snatch away any moment. He has discussed death and the ephemeral nature of the body at considerable length since a true estimate of this physical structure is essential for eliminating egotism.

THE FALLACY OF PLEASURE

Then he exposes the fallacy of pleasure. It (pleasure) is only a passing sensation which cannot survive separation of contact between the respective sense and its object of agreeability. To seek happiness in pleasure is to give external objects—over which we have little or no control, and which are equally ephemeral and unreal like the human body—the power to disturb your peace. "Pleasure is neither good nor useful", he says.

Next he proceeds to examine the nature of happiness which is and should rightly be our motive for living and comes to the mind which transcends all ideas of dualities like pain and pleasure, heat and cold, joy and sorrow.

He also examines the means to attain happiness and decides that the prime requisite is renunciation which consists of contentment, non-attachment for one's family and belongings and distaste for temporal pleasures. "Abstain from desire in any form.......", cautions the Roman Emperor.

There are within all of us both the lower and higher (divine) natures existing side by side—the first depending on ignorance and selfishness and the second, on knowledge and selflessness. We must outgrow the fomer and nourish and strengthen the latter. "Dig within thee. There lies the fount of good, a fount whose waters will for ever well up if thou but ever dig.' Realise your status in relation to the universe. "Let this thought be ever present in thee: that the universe is a single life, comprising one substance and one soul. Observe how all things have reference to this universal perception, all acting with a single impulse, all co-factors in the creation of all that is, and all threads indissolubly united in one web."

The mind, which is both our friend and foe, plays innumerable tricks on us. Seek the friend and throw out the enemy in you. Make it your ally in your "pilgrimage of life." Have control over thoughts and desires because they are the stuff the mind is made of. "Wipe away every alien, disturbing thought and straightaway enter the great calm." Fix your thoughts on God, who is the abode of all that is noble and good.

Next, sink your egotism in the service of your brethren. "Men exist for mutual service." Eschew all thoughts of reward or profit in your action. "Realize the purpose of life...... Earthly existence yields but one harvest, holiness of character and altruism in action..........." "Make for the shortest path, which is Nature; in other words, healthiness in speech and action. For a man with this purpose, life is freed from all vexation."

With the dawn of true knowledge, which is not mere possession of information, but indicates living in conformity with the highest truth, man establishes his link and identity with the Supreme Being. Just as a mirror cleansed of all blemish reflects flawlessly, a life purged of all impurities reflects the Supreme. In this state, all shackles are broken and man is liberated.

We need not be frightened by the heights to be scaled. Concentrate on this moment, leaving the rest to God. "Be content with the smallest progress made, remembering that this consummation is no small thing," says Marcus Aurelius.

As has been said of another great work on spiritual life, it can be truly stated of the 'Meditations', that "with its perennial applicability, it provides with a singularity of breath for every stage of human evolution and has something to teach every man that makes him better and purer."

Note : This chapter is an adaptation of the essay which won for the author the First Prize in an open contest on 'Meditations of Marcus Aurelius.' Two eminent Indian University Professors of Philosophy acted as Judges.

❑❑

13

HOW TO BE THE MASTER OF YOUR CIRCUMSTANCES

"No discovery of modern psychology is, in my opinion, so important as its scientific proof of the necessity of self-sacrifice or discipline to self-realisation and happiness."

— Dr. Henry C. Link

THE TEACHINGS OF SAINTS & PROPHETS

The scriptures and other religious and spiritual literature serve as teachers and guides of man. Besides showing the path to perfection, they unveil to us the real nature of our- selves, remove doubts about our weaknesses and give us confidence in our strength. Great books in this category are really the teachings of saints, prophets and sages who speak to us through their pages.

A pregnant lioness, while pouncing upon a flock of sheep, suddenly gave birth to a cub and died, leaving its little one in the midst of the sheep. Growing among the grass-eating lambs, the lion cub imagined itself to be a lamb, lived on grass, bleated like a lamb and took fright on seeing carnivorous wild beasts. One day a big lion happened again to attack the flock, but was surprised to see the strange, lamb-like behaviour of a young lion. It caught hold of the little one and chided it: "You eat grass, bleat like a lamb and run away frightened like the sheep. You are a disgrace to the race of lions. Come, roar like me. Eat this piece of meat and live with me hereafter." But the cub could not believe or trust the big one and began bleating again like a lamb helplessly.

Then the lion forcibly took the young one to a nearby stream and roared: "Look at your reflection and realise that you are a lion and not a lamb." The cub was taken aback at this revelation. Thereafter it followed the big lion and gradually came to live according to its true nature, that of a lion.

Teachers and scriptures are like the grown up lion in the story. Like the cub we feel weak, inadequate and lack the confidence to face life. At every turn we are frightened and wish to run away. In other words, the majority of us feels that we are creatures of circumstances. And one of the unique books extant, the 'Imitation of Christ' tells us point blank that we need not feel this limitation and can become the masters of our circumstances. Man is a miserable creature and slave to his passions as long as he does not assert not only his liberty, but his mastery. Now let Kempis speak:

> *"Son, thou must diligently make it thy aim, that in every action, or outward employment, thou be inwardly* ***free*** *and* ***Master of Thyself and that All Things be under Thee and Not Thou Under Them."***
>
> ***"That Thou Mayst be Lord and Ruler of Thy Actions,*** *not a slave or bondsman."*

How can you be inwardly free and master of thyself and "all things be under thee"? Here is the answer:

> *"Son, thou canst not possess perfect liberty* ***Unless Thou Wholly deny Thyself."***
>
> **— Matth. XVA. 24**
>
> *"All self-seekers and self-lovers are bound in fetters, full of desires, full of cares, un-settled and seeking always their own ease, and not the things of Jesus Christ. Phil.III.21 but often times devising and framing that which will not stand.*
>
> *"This vice, by which a man inordinately loves himself, is at the bottom of all that which is to be rooted out and overcome in thee; which evil being once conquered and brought under, a great peace and tranquility will presently ensue."*

"But there are few that labour ***to die perfectly to themselves*** *and that fully aim beyond themselves, therefore do they remain entangled in themselves, nor can they be elevated in spirit above themselves."*

"Take this short and perfect word: ***Forsake all And thou Shall find All, Leave Thy desires and Thou Shalt Find Rest."***

"If thou perfectly overcome thyself, thou shalt with more Ease subdue all Things Else."

How is one to overcome oneself perfectly, how to forsake all, how to wholly deny oneself?

"He that is ***wise and well instructed in spirit*** *stands above all these changes; not minding what he feels in himself, not on what side the wind of instability blows; but that the whole bent of his soul may advance towards his due and wished-for end."*

"For so he may continue one and the self-same without being shaken, by directing without ceasing, through all this variety of events, ***The single eye of his intention towards me.***

— Matth. VI. 22

"Any by How much purer the eye of the intention is, with so much greater constancy mayst thou pass through these diverse storms."

"The eye of the intention therefore must be purified that it may be single and right, and must be Directed to me, Beyond all the various objects that interpose themselves."

Now the key sentences in the whole scheme are:

"Thou canst not possess perfect liberty unless thou wholly deny thyself" and

"If thou perfectly overcome thyself"

> *"He that is wise and well-instructed in spirit stands above all changes,"*
>
> *"So he may continue one and the self-same....... by directing **without ceasing**, the single eye of his intention towards me."*

all of which amounts to complete self-surrender to God and abjuration of everything selfish which alone will give you complete **"Mastery of Thyself, Render all Things under thee, and Give you control over Circumstances."**

We have had occasion previously to refer to the curious phenomenon of man who forsakes all finding all. **The alchemy of Self-Sacrifice!**

A well-known Sanskrit couplet rendered freely reads thus:

> *"It is not through wealth, progeny or anything, but through renunciation alone a few have attained immortality",*

And another poet says:

> *"In enjoyment, there is the fear of disease; in social position, the fear of falling off; in wealth, the fear of kings (i.e., taxes); in honour, the fear of humiliation; in power, the fear of enemies; in beauty, the fear of old age; in scriptural erudition, the fear of opponents; in virtue, the fear of traducers; in body, the fear of death. All things of this world are attended with fear; **Renunciation Alone stands For fearlessness.**"*

The same bard has said:

> *"The objects of enjoyments will leave us one by one, sooner or later. (We cannot retain them permanently with us). Actually their loss should not make any difference as we will be forced to abandon them. If we give them up reluctantly, it brings affliction of mind. Whereas if we renounce them willingly of our own accord, that act of renunciation conduces to bliss and self-possession."*

One of world's greatest men of recent past, Mahatma Gandhi, wielded immense power over men and shaped the destiny of a sub-continent with a single weapon: renunciation—absolute selflessness. This can come only to a man who has steadfast faith in God—'whose single eye of his intention is directed towards ME.'

Indeed Gandhi was the poorest of the poor, but by choice. When Gandhi died, Louis Fischer wrote: "Humanity was impoverished because a poor man had died." You might have read the moving biography of this unusual man, written with perfect sincerity and complete understanding by such eminent American writers like Louis Fischer (*Gandhi, the Man and His Mission*), Dr. John Haynes Holmes (*My Gandhi*) and Vincent Sheean (*Lead Kindly Light*). It is a tribute to the greatness of the human spirit that Gandhi's life and mission have so well been studied, understood and narrated by men of other faiths and other lands. I would go a step further and state that Gandhi was better understood by men and women outside his own country. The extraordinary life of the Mahatma* could as well be summed up in one word: "Renunciation."

Note : The phenomenal success of Attenburough's film 'Gandhi' which went on to win nine Oscars is yet another witness of the Mahatma's appeal to people all over the world.

❑❑

---

*Literally, "Great soul."

14

THE ABODE OF GOD

" Know ye not that ye are the temple of God, and that spirit of God dwelleth in you."

I Cor. 3:16

THE SIMILARITIES IN RELIGIOUS LITERATURES

It is very interesting to see similarities in religious literature of different lands and languages. Thomas a Kempis in his "Imitation of Christ" writes: "Christ will come to thee, discovering to thee His consolation, *if thou wilt prepare Him a fit dwelling within thee.*"

Reminding one of this, there is a moving passage in the Ramayana, the great Hindu epic (of which there are several versions) in which Rama, the incarnation of God, the hero, has a conversation with Valmiki, the sage and the original author of the epic. Coming to stay in the forests, Rama asks the sage if he could suggest a suitable place for Him to reside. Valmiki is overwhelmed at this naive question of the Lord, and gives a magnificent description of what could constitute a "suitable abode for Him' in the following lines which is a free prose rendering of the original:

Those who are calm, and possessed of equal vision, never hate any being and always contemplate you

—Their heart is thy beautiful dwelling place.

Forgetting all considerations of right and wrong, who remember you always
— Their heart will be the ideal home for you and your consort, Sita.

Repeating Thy holy name, who come to you in utter self-surrender; who have transcended dualities, who have no selfish desires whatsoever
— Their heart shall be a sweet home for Thee.

Those who live devoid of egotism, avoid likes and dislikes, view a clod of earth and a piece of gold alike
— Their heart shall be Thy celestial home.

Surrendering their mind and intellect to Thee, who remain always contented and dedicate the results of their actions to Thee
— Their heart is Thy holy abode.

Those who do not despond at unfavourable events, nor rejoice on attaining favourable results, and reminding themselves of the illusory and transitory nature of everything in this world, contemplate You always
— Their heart is Thy sacred residence.

Viewing birth, growth, decay and death as the attributes of this physical body and not of the Soul; hunger, thirst, pleasure and pain as relating to life breath; they who are liberated from the tentacles of mundane existence
— Their heart is Thy holy residence.

Who always rejoice seeing You as permeating everything, realising Your nature as Existence-Intelligence-Bliss absolute, changeless and one without a second, without beginning or end, Supreme
— There, in the lotus of their hearts do Thou reside with Your bride.

Strengthening their will by unceasing practice, established in the worship of Thy holy feet, who by constant chanting of Thy holy name, have destroyed all their sins
— In their heart, with Sita Your consort do make your retreat.

Concluding, the great Sage-poet exclaims:

How can I, O Rama, state, much less describe, the greatness of Thy holy name, by the alchemy of which I attained exalted sainthood?

(***Note:*** Valmiki who was originally a highway robber underwent a transformation and, initiated into penance by chanting Rama's name constantly, became a revered sage. The story of his transformation is given in a subsequent chapter.)

❑❑

15

HOW TO FACE AND DEAL WITH ADVERSE CRITICISM AND SLANDER

"When any one has offended me, I try to raise my soul so high that the offence cannot reach it."

— Descartes

THE FEELING OF 'I' AND 'MINE' — A DISEASE COMMON TO ALL

Even with the best of intentions and true sincerity, it is not always passible to push the world out of your life. People around you will not leave you to your ways even if you do not intrude into theirs. We have in many ways to adjust ourselves to the people about us. In other words, we should be in this world, yet not of it.

The best amongst us, the truly noble and consciencious, cannot hope to sail on the sea of life free form the hazards of the storm of wilful criticism and slander. It is indeed an inexplicable quirk or human nature that we take to a painstaking and close scrutiny of others' actions and character with missionary zeal and their failings (imaginary, real or cooked up), than their better traits catch our eye. We have to derive consolation form the fact that few can escape calumny, however innocent, highly placed or mighty one might be. As Shakespeare has said:

"Be thou as chaste as ice, as pure, as snow, Thou shall not escape calumny,"

— Hamlet III, 1

And again,

"No might, nor greatness in mortality
Can censure 'scape ; back-wounding calumny
The whitest virtue strikes. What king so strong
Can tie the gall up on the slanderous tongue?

— Measure for Measure, Act III Scene II

"Rumour is a pipe
Blown by surmises, jealousies, conjectures".

— Henry IV, Scene II

"Whose edge is sharper than the sword, whose tongue
outvenoms all the worms of Nile, whose breath
Rides on the posting winds and doth belie
All corners of the world: kings, queens and states,
Maids, matrons, nay, the secrets of the grave
This viperous slander enters."

— Cymbeline, III, 4

Is it not mysterious that most of us should be found guilty, sometime or the other, of having indulged ourselves in this slanderous pastime, all the time conscious that we have often nothing to gain and the victim a lot to lose? Who can put it better than Shakespeare?

"Who steals my purse, steals trash;
It is some thing, nothing;
But he that filches from me my good name
Robs me of that which not enriches him,
And makes me poor indeed."

— Othello

While we have heard quite a lot about unostentatious performance of good deeds and religious practices, it is indeed very, very difficult to get over the weakness of desire to win a good name, the approval and approbation of our fellow-men, and particularly of those who are not kindly disposed towards us. This urge is a powerful motive and is at the bottom of most 'good deeds'. Giving alms, donations, undertaking social work, all generally calculated to get appreciation and fame. There is no limit to which certain people would go to earn popularity. From worldly stand point, this craving for popularity is quite useful and but for it, many of the institutions which owe their origin and continuance to the munificence of rich patrons would not have been there. For those few who do not really care for this applause, good and pious deeds should serve as means for achieving humility, self discipline or mortification of the flesh in an effort to transcend that disease common to all, the feeling of 'I' and 'mine'. This is the reason for the emphasis placed by religious leaders on the need for unostentation.

Why do I deal with the desire for popularity while talking about how to face criticism? Because the two are closely linked. Not getting appreciation or approbation is itself painful, then how much more grievous should criticism appear ? But unless we deal with it in the appropriate manner, we are likely not only to suffer but also go astray in an effort to silence it. One common mistake most of us are likely to commit in the face of adverse comment is to try to pacify, placate or even bribe (figuratively and literally) the critic. In our anxiety to silence him, we are actually rewarding the slanderer if we give out the slightest sign of notice. The very idea that it is having its effect is enough to gladden his heart. On the top of it, if we are going to bribe him, that is the limit, for we are just succumbing to his blackmail! We have to be indifferent not only to criticism if it is unjust, but to flattery as well, in both of which the other person is concerned only with what he can get out of us or how to get form us what he wants. Both are used for exploitation. "Be hearty in your approbation and lavish in your praise," exhorts the popularity expert. To what end? Either to get what you want from the recipient or to win popularity for yourself. The path indicated by the expert is of course very unselfish! He wheedles you to be satisfied even with creating just *goodwill alone*, which is one of the ways of becoming popular, isn't it? Now reverse the advice of the expert: "Be hearty in your condemnation and lavish in your criticism!" I think this formula can secure for you equally good results if the victim succumbs (as people usually do) to the blackmailer. Fear is a very potent weapon and playing on this emotion is fully effective in "influencing" people.

DEALING WITH CRITICISM AND SLANDER

There is no better method of dealing with criticism and slander than which is enjoined in our scriptures: Be equally indifferent to praise as well as blame-but only on one condition: you have taken all possible care and pains to see that your actions are based on pure foundations. Where the criticism is justified, it should be welcomed and in its light we should correct ourselves. That is the positive aspect of genuine, helpful criticism. Where it is unjust and unjustified, we should recall what *The Imitation of Christ* says:

> *"Let not thy peace be in the tongues of men, for whether they put a good or bad construction of what thou dost, thou are not for all that other than what thou art. Where is true peace and true glory? Is it not in Me?"*
>
> *"And he who seeks not to please men, nor fears their displeasure, shall enjoy much peace - Col. III. 22. All disquiet of heart and distraction of the senses arise from inordinate love and vain fear.* Fear God, and thou shalt have no need of being afraid of man."*
>
> *"Many say many things and therefore little credit is to be given to them. Neither is it possible to satisfy all."*
>
> *"Son, cast thy heart firmly on the Lord, and fear not the judgement of man when thy conscience gives testimony to thy piety and innocence."*
>
> *"As long as suffering** appear grievous to thee and thou seekest to fly from it, so long will it be ill with thee, and the tribulation from which thou fliest will everywhere follow thee."*

---

* Should we add 'inordinate love of praise and vain fear of censure'?

** In the present context, suffering on account of slander or adverse comment.

We can with benefit reproduce here Abe Lincoln's famous reply to those who urged him to repudiate unjust criticism about him and his administration:

> *"If I were to try to read, much less to answer, all the attacks made on me, this shop might as well be closed for any other business. I do the very best I know how — the very best I can; and I mean to keep on doing so until the end. If the end brings me out all right, then what is said against me won't matter. If the end bring me out wrong, then ten angels swearing I was right would make no difference."*

Since the aim of this book is to press into service the collective wisdom of the ancients as well as moderns as far as it is possible in our effort to live the higher life, I reproduce below the wise observation of a great modern minister, Harry Emerson Fosdick:

> *"Many people are extremely touchy about criticism. Sensitivity to the opinion of others, without which social life could not exist at all, has in them been perverted into a disease. Such abnormal people take appreciation for granted and regard criticism as an impertinence. The normal person comes nearer to taking criticism for granted and regarding appreciation as a "**bonus.**"*

❑❑

16

PATHS TO HOLINESS—I

"Whether therefore ye eat, or drink, or whatsoever ye do, do all to the glory of God."

— I Cor. 10:31

NOURISHING THE HOLINESS

We have seen wise Marcus Aurelius declare: "Earthly existence yields but one harvest, holiness of character and altruism in action........" Holiness is not an end, but only the means. It is not an outward manifestation but an inward condition. It is not to be got for the mere asking. It has its price. It calls for discipline, watchfulness and diligent practice.

For Christmas we get up the Christmas tree and decorate our houses for the festival. In their absence we are not likely to *feel* the atmosphere of this particular festival of rejoicing. On the contrary, if there is a death in a family, we can easily make out the same from the dress and bearing of the bereaved. An aristocrat makes his presence in his neighbourhood felt by having luxurious limousines, palatial bungalows, carefully laid-out gardens, tastefully decorated interiors and so on.

Similarly, if we wish to nourish holiness in our thoughts and actions and through them in our lives, we have to live in the proper atmosphere. I do not mean that every one living the higher life should take to the proverbial 'sack cloth and ashes.' But luxurious living with its accent on outward appearance can hardly be in consonance with the life in the spirit. We associate godliness not only with cleanliness but also with simplicity and unostentation. The outward appearance of our person, habiliment and habitation has to be attuned to the religious life equally with our inner condition.

The *Bhagavat Gita*, the holy scripture of the Hindus, sets out the attributes of holiness, the qualities which distinguish a holy man from a worldly man, as follows:

> *Humility, unpretentiousness, non-injuriousness,*
> *Peacefulness, uprightness:*
> *Service to the holy and the preceptor;*
> *Purity, steadfastness, self-control;*
> *Aversion to sense-pleasures, absence of egotism;*
> *Constant reflections on the evils of birth, death, senility, disease and pain;*
> *Non-identification (detachment) of self with son, wife, home and the rest;*
> *Unruffled, uniform even-mindedness in pleasant and unpleasant occurences;*
> *Unswerving devotion to God, resort to solitude, distaste for the company of worldly-minded men;*
> *Assiduous application to spiritual knowledge, understanding the real purpose of knowledge and what is true knowledge:*
> *These are the paths to holiness; anything else can only lead to ignorance and suffering.*

Note the skilful blending of outward observances with inward culture. The list is rather forbidding, no doubt, but one can discern the central theme running through them all, namely these qualities of the head and heart which uplift instead of degrading.

There can be many roads leading to the same destination. Similarly religious practices need not be stereotyped and uniform. Disciplines like fasting, common to most religions, tend to tame the rebellious flesh whose craving, if a man is out to satisfy, will invariably end in a wild-goose-chase. But extremes in mortifications are to be avoided as they defeat their purpose by centering our attention unduly on this body.

We have already dealt with the need for rendering service to our fellow-men, seeing them as various forms of the one

God. That also helps us to forget ourselves by engaging our body and mind in work which alleviates human suffering or ministers to the needs of others.

All religions lay great stress on charity. It can truly be said that the poor help us when we help them because we do not expect any return from them nor are they in a position to repay. Charity fosters not only self-sacrifice but also a feeling of identity with others, especially the less fortunate.

It goes without saying that if we wish to cultivate noble qualities, we must associate with people with similar bent of mind and *avoid* the company of those who have scant regard for them. When like-minded people gather, naturally their coversation will centre round topics of common interest. Some of the world's great religions have emphasised the need for association with holy men. We admire those who are of superior calibre and this admiration paves the way for our unconscious assimilation of their ideals and conscious emulation of their ways. We are often guided by great souls if we humbly seek their help. Here I cannot but recall the moving account of Vincent Sheean of his visit to Gandhi and how be felt he was helped by the saint - not only in life, but even after his death.

REMEMBERING THE GOD

It is also necessary to remember God constantly while going about our allotted daily tasks. This is made easy by our repeating God's name. We can make God our constant companion; we can talk to Him, consult Him, demand His help and guidance, even force Him if we but hold Him bound to us through our love for Him. Religious literature often finds worldly experiences handy and useful to drive home great religious truths to the common man in an understandable language. Thus the incessant remembrance of God by the devotee is compared to the rapturous recollection by a woman, in illicit love, of her paramour. She may go about her daily chores in her usual way, but she ever carries in her consciousness a picture of her beloved — his amorous conversation, his face and features and what not. Similarly, whatever be his pre-occupation, the devote never for a moment loses hold of God-consciousness.

In India there is a popular form of mass entertainment in which a scholar narrates in popular language, with the aid of music stories from the epics and mythology which are invariably God-oriented. This mass remembrance of God, which occasionally takes the from of chorus singing of God's glories, calls to mind the Biblical statement :

> *"For where two or three are gathered together in My name, there am I in the midst of them....."*
>
> ***— Chapter 18 of the Gospel according to Matthew***

Members of the audience not infrequently develop a fervour, their frames shake with thrills, they shed tears of joy, experience horripilation and even swoon during such recitals.

As has been pointed out in another chapter, the common man cannot conceive of any enjoyment superior to those which his senses can procure for him. Until he is led step by step to higher levels of joy which are super-sensual, we cannot laugh at him if he swears by the testimony of his senses. The starting point in the higher life is faith; faith in God, faith in the higher life and faith in the existence of higher forms of joy. It is the duty of the enlightened to educate the masses gradually and the religious gathering referred to, serve as the media of such education. Westerners visiting India would do well to take pains to study the techniques of mass religious instruction employed by the Hindus where there is little *direct* preaching or sermonising. It is seldom that a direct or blunt reference is made to the so-called sinfulness of man. There is more remembrance and recollection of God and His greatness and in this process this sordid worldly existence is at least temporarily forgotten. The listener identifies himself with the trials and tribulations of a soul in its Godward ascent, inflicted by an understanding society or king. Ultimately in such stories, devotion and piety triumph, thus establishing the invincibility of God and His righteousness.

❑❑

17

PATHS TO HOLINESS—II

"Complete the pilgrimage through life as one who has wholeheartedly entrusted all things to Heaven"

— Marcus Aurelius

PILGRIMAGES—THE THREE DISTINCT CONSTITUENTS

Now we shall deal with another discipline common to most religions : pilgrimages.

Pilgrims, as we know, are persons who journey to sacred places as an act of devotion. Marcus Aurelius conceives this life itself as a pilgrimage. In America, the legend of the Pilgrim Fathers has particular significance. Every religion has its places of pilgrimage — Jerusalem, Mecca, Benares, Bodh Gaya and many others. It is also a common feature of almost all religions that they enjoin on their followers to undertake such journeys and believe in their sacredness. Hindu monks, during a certain stage, have to live in continuous pilgrimages as they are prohibited from staying in a single place for more than a few days.

A pilgrimage has three distinct constituents : the pilgrim, the place of pilgrimage and the act of pilgrimage. The sanctity of a particular place depends on faith and sentiment. Many stories are built around such places to distinguish them from others. In the mind of the person undertaking a pilgrimage, there is the picture of the pilgrim centre as a holy place with associations of holy men and their holy acts.

A pilgrimage really originates in the mind of the prospective pilgrim. First there is the hankering, a driving desire to go on a pilgrimage. Secondly, once the place is decided, it exerts a powerful influence over his imagination. Generally, the place selected is a far-off one, not easily accessible. Many days of journeying is involved and in olden days this journeying had to be done mostly on foot. When one has to be away for a number of days, even months, one's worldly possessions and estates have to be entrusted to other's care. Thus there is a detachment from the cares of day-to-day living. In those days of long journeying, one could hardly equip oneself with requirements of food for the entire journey. Therefore one had to be prepared to face privations on the way, if necessary.

From the time one contemplates it, the pilgrimage occupies one's thought most of the time. As days pass by, it develops into a fervour. One thinks less and less of other things and more and more of the sacred place. Could one reach it, and stand face to face the sanctum sanctorum? What would happen if something occurred to cause one to abandon the trip? Many such anxieties grip the prospective pilgrim. But such anxiety is an elevating one unlike the cares of the daily life in this world.

Then there is often a certain penance enjoined before and during the journey. Some religions have conventions of fasting, continence, meditation in the form of repetition of God's name, restrictions as to the colour of one's dress, prohibition of shave or haircut for the duration and many others. One must take a vow to give up at least one vice or bad habit. One pilgrim should not refuse any reasonable request of a fellow pilgrim.

THE IDEA BEHIND THE PILGRIMAGES

What might be the idea behind such pilgrimages? One can reasonably conclude that they constitute a probation in higher thinking and in spiritual, selfless living. The functions of the body, mind and intellect and thus the soul's are attuned to a higher life. All the habitual weaknesses, meanness, selfishness are abandoned for a time. He helps, he is helped. In effect, he gives the new mode of living a trial. Standing face to face the sanctum sanctorum is the hour of triumph of the soul or spirit over the flesh. This consummation devoutly desired and achieved, the pilgrim returns to his place and to his normal living. Will it fail to leave an indelible impress on his life thereafter ?

There are many excellent books recording pilgrims' experiences. Bunyon's *The Pilgrim's Progress* is unfortunately (or fortunately?) an allegory. There is the beautiful story by Count Leo Tolstoy about "Two Old Men" on a pilgrimage to Jerusalem. One should not miss to read it - it is so simple yet full of significance. An unusual record of miraculours experiences, which is of great interest to the religious as well as the secular, is a famous scientist's account of another pilgrimage: *A Journey to Lourdes* by Dr. Alexis Carrel who accompanied a patient in the advanced stages of tuberculosis, to Lourdes, the famous pilgrim centre and scene of many a miracle. It was actually a fact-finding trip of young Carrel. As Dr. A.J. Cronin has remarked, medical men seldom start as believers. Therefore Dr. Carrel's account and convictions are all the more weighty. The miraculous cure, of which he was an eye witness, opened his eyes and led him to a conviction about the unsurpassed power of prayer* which he has shared with others in a series of writings on the subject.

❑❑

---

* See Appendix *C*.

18

NEW IDEAS OR OLD

Knowledge comes, but wisdom lingers

—The Bible

All change is not progress.
All knowledge is not wisdom.

—Abraham Lincoln

THE REVERENCE FOR EVERYTHING ON EARTH

You might have heard of the great epic of the Hindus, the Mahabharata, a reference to which has been made earlier. It is the story of an ancient warrior race of India. The chiefs of the two clans, Yudhistira and Duryodhana were studies in contrast and there are many anecdotes illustrating their respective mental outlook. A couple of them narrated below would be illuminating.

When both of them were students, their teacher, Drona, had ample reasons to be partial to the mild and straightforward Yudhistira which brought forth continual protests from Dritarashtra, the blind father of Duryodhana and uncle of Yudhistira. The preceptor wanted to demonstrate if his preference was not justified. One day in the presence of the blind king, each of the two princes was given a gold coin separately without the knowledge of the other. They were asked to spend the money and fill a room allotted to each which was vacant and dark. Without hesitation Duryodhana went to the market place, bought a few cart-loads of hay with the money and filled the room shown to him. Whereas the other prince bought a neat little lamp and some oil which he lit and filled the room allotted to him with light.

On another occasion, a test was again given to the two princes. Duryodhana was called first and asked to go around among his friends and acquaintances and fetch a man who was his superior in learning or looks or prowess. He took little time and returned triumphantly to announce that his mission had ended in total failure; he could not find a single man who was *superior* to him in any respect. Then the other prince was summoned and given a similar assignment, but of a different, opposite type - he was asked to find a person *inferior* to him. The boy earnestly searched the entire capital city and he too reported complete failure. He could find none *inferior* to him.

You would have drawn the moral. Many Westerners have visited the Indian sub-continent and several have recorded their observations—their discoveries of India. At one extreme you find the well-known Miss Mayo who threw up her hands in holy horror at the wretchedness and total lack of decency in that country. Gandhi humourously characterised her book: "A drain inspector's report." Others have taken a middle-of-the road stand: they found something good and something bad. That is quite understandable. But a few found nothing very repugnant except the abject poverty of the masses and did find something worth appreciating, even emulating. In this last category comes Vincent Sheean who has shown keen insight, sincerity and open-mindedness in his book on Gandhi, *Lead Kindly Light*. He has not laboured hard to give a new meaning or twist to some of the sordid things that do exist in the ancient land of India. He shows great penetration in assessing the significance of several aspects of the life of the Hindu, especially in his reading of the meaning of the phenomenon of *Darshan* which reveals his earnest desire to understand the Indian mind. In my opinion, even Sheean has failed to notice one great trait in the life and thought of the Hindus. It is *reverence*, reverence not only for life but for almost everything on earth.

If the cow and the monkey are sacred animals to the Hindu, the snake is a sacred reptile, a mendicant minstrel is sacred and if it surprises a visitor, it is because the stranger does not know that these are only a few of the one thousand-and-one things which are sacred for the followers of Hinduism. A banyan tree is sacred. Water is sacred. A river is sacred. The poor man is *Daridra Narayana* — God in the form of the poor. A guest, the preceptor, father, mother, they are all gods, a well known convocation address appended to the ancient Vedas (sacred text of the Hindus) declares. Before embarking on any venture, people pay respects to elders by prostrating before them and seek their blessings for success. Indeed not only are animate and inanimate beings held in reverence, but almost every function of the human body is sacred, too. Eating is sanctified by offering food first to the Gods. Bathing is sanctified by an imaginary dip in the river Ganges which is, of course, holy of holies. Singing is sacred and till the advent of the modern motion picture, songs were all 'kirtans,' hymns sung about the glory of the Lord. Dancing - Indian style, which is entirely different from what goes by that name in the West—is *abhinaya* or acting, depicting the various episodes in the Divine Sport.

Even a sensual, biological function like sexual intercourse is sacred—there is a special religious ceremony apart from the marriage rituals, to initiate the newly wed in the *holy act* of *Garbha-dan*, that is, gifting a progeny. And another sacred text enjoins, among other things, to "visualize progeny, joy and immortality in the organs of procreation." But what is not so obvious to the foreigner is that the sublime sentiment of reverence arises from an outlook which sees the one God in all life, sentient or insentient, all activity and all matter-in short, everything.

This attitude permeated the life of the ancient Hindus so completely that unscrupulous foreigners got a foothold on their land which was the beginning of empires of several alien invaders, marauders and traders. Yet this reverence enabled the Hindus to achieve an incomparably harmonious blending of the religious and the secular. The consequence has been that even the poorest had a glow of contentment, an unmistakable, if faint, glimmer of independent happiness in an otherwise wretched secular existence. And Hinduism as a religion has survived all vicissitudes. The inroads made by other civilisations into India's ancient culture have started being felt and at a not too distant future the life of the Hindu, even the ignorant and illiterate, promises to become a mad race for material wealth and physical comfort to the detriment, nay abandoning, of his strangely contented existence. There is no use being nostalgic, as every 'progress' takes its toll and one cannot long to hold on to the old modes of living as years roll by!

FOUR 'ENDS' OF HUMAN LIFE

Another concept of the Hindus is the four 'ends' of human life — *purushartha*. A man must strive for four things in life. They are righteousness or virtue (which has been given the first place as has been done in the Bible—"seek ye first the Kingdom of God"), material prosperity, legitimate enjoyment of sense pleasure and lastly, liberation or final absorption into Godhead. They no doubt overlap. A grown-up man endeavours simultaneously to achieve all the four 'ends,' though gradually. Within the limits of righteousness and aspiration for liberation, the other two should be pursued. Material prosperity enables one to be upright himself and of service to his fellows. Man must quench his thirst for sense pleasures, otherwise his mind will continue to dwell on them, hindering his progress, 'Know, enjoy, exhaust and proceed'.

Coming on the heels of the previous idea is the division of a man's life into four *ashramas* or stages. They are the continent, austere life of a student, then that of a householder (married life with service to one's family and community distinguishing it), thirdly, living a retired life (generally in the forest) preparing oneself for the last state, namely the life of an anchorite. This formal division is for the average man as there had been many instances of a young student skipping the intervening two stages and launching himself as an ascetic straightway.

I wonder if this division of life into stages has not a relevance to modern times. Students should devote themselves exclusively to their studies. Are they doing so now? A certain rigid discipline enforced on young students in their formative years lays the foundation for a balanced life of the grown-up when observance of more difficult self-control becomes less taxing due to the prior training.

It is also necessary to embark on married life immediately the young are *physically fit* or mature. Present-day civilization, so the authorities in modern medicine and psychology aver, delays marriage too much, thus a great strain in placed on the young in observing pre-marital continence and chastity and the married woman becomes a mother rather late, later than the period when she is best equipped by nature to do so.

As for retired life — except for government servants and employees at the lower levels — is there an age of superannuation prevalent now? Particularly for the successful businessman, who is his own boss, is there a power that can make him retire? You may ask why a man should retire when he is willing to work for a longer period. Why should government employees have such a stipulation? There are many reasons, and one particularly which is not quite secular. Once a man is released from the necessity of working to earn a livelihood, he can devote himself to the service of his community and God better and more intensively. All may not like to enter the next stage, that of an ascetic. As a matter of fact, none may. A man has lived a full life and arrived at a stage when not many things, which previously used to, can give him the same satisfaction in enjoyment any longer. With the advent of old age, a man should deliberately seek to slow down and curb his turbulence because his energy cannot be taxed at the same rate as before. He has to find satisfaction and joy on a different level altogether. Can there be any joy, especially for an elderly man, equal to that of the pursuit of the higher life of the intellect and spirit? His Maker will call him back one day, sooner than later. Would he not like to depart with the satisfaction of having put his things and affairs in order, with a heart and mind bent on, and looking forward to, meeting Him? Are weightier arguments needed for preparing for such a glorious end, which life in retirement should really amount to? Unless one retires from business or profession at the right time, can such consummation ever be achieved?*

The line that divides the orthodox and heterodox, the religious and the secular, the scientific and the superstitious, is indeed a thin one. We can never cut asunder from our past and attach ourselves to the future at one stroke. It is a steady progression, past, present and future. And in reality there are no such distinctions in eternity. But where does the modern man have time to reflect? That is indeed to repeat the tragedy of our times!

❑❑

* See Appendix *F.*

19

A SONG OF THE SOUL

Though earth and moon were gone,
And sun and universes ceased to be,
And Thou wert left alone,
Every existence would exist in Thee.

— Emily Bronte

THE LIFE PRINCIPLE IS SAME IN EVERYONE

The ordinary conversation language of man (irrespective of nationality or religion) has a mysterious capacity to unveil profound religious and philosophical truths. To illustrate : While we talk about the various constituent members, i.e., limbs or senses, of our body, we always refer to them as something separate, something distinct from ourselves. 'This is my hand, ' 'my leg,' 'my heart', 'my mind' and so on. Each one of them, it is clear, is not myself. Otherwise I would not refer to them in such terms. When a man dies, his *body* (mortal remains, in elegant language) is buried or cremated. If these several units, body, mind, intellect, are not 'me' or 'I', who then am I? Obviously the Soul, not merely the breath. Only in its presence does a man remain a live man, else he is a corpse.

Now a little reflection will convince us that even though beings appear separate, the life principle is same in every one. How is it? In your home you have various electrical gadgets: lights, cooking range, the fridge, fans, the TV set and others. For all these instruments, the power behind is electrical energy which is invisible to the eye. A power failure renders all these various apparatus as "dead." So electrical energy activating these different gadgets is the same in each of them. Fires may be separate in every hearth, but fire is same everywhere. Similarly, the life principle which is behind all animate and inanimate beings is one. That is variously called the 'Divine Ground', 'Tao,' 'Atman', 'Self' and so on.

It we can unmistakably recognize that the 'Divine Ground' is the common prime-mover in all of us whether we belong to the bird, animal or plant kingdom or human species, we can at once establish that the whole universe is basically one, eliminating ideas of separateness. Then all conflicts will cease.

Great religions proclaim that we sin or err only when our acts are motivated by thoughts or *'duality' or 'separateness.'* Few doubt the existence of God, but it is not easy to see the same God in every one of us, even theoretically. Practice is still more difficult. Yet real knowledge consists of this realisation.

For those who have not reached this summit of knowledge, it is very difficult, if not impossible to conceive of God without form, and still more difficult to describe a God without form. Once you set out to define or describe, you impose limitations whereas God is limitless, infinite.* That is why oriental seers resorted to a method of negation instead of assertion, God is 'not this' 'not that.' He is not like this, nor like that. By this process of elimination or exclusion, they arrived at the conclusion that the Divine Ground is 'Existence-Knowledge-Bliss' absolute. He is referred to as He in His personal aspect and It in His Impersonal aspect. *It* is Existence absolute because It is the sub-stratum of all life. It is Knowledge absolute because It is the Entity in every being, the Witness, the Pure Consciousness which knows that you do know or do not know. It is Bliss absolute because joy or bliss in whatever form any being experiences is only a glimpse or minute particle of that ocean of joy, that Joy absolute. There is no birth, death or change for It.

---

* "If He could be pinned down with a few adjectives, He would no longer be God."

— Warren Weaver

SOUL—THE PARTICLE OF THE DIVINE GROUND

It is not this body, mind, intellect or ego that gives us undying bliss. It is only the Soul which again is a particle of the Universal Soul, the Divine Ground. If we want to search for the abode of eternal bliss and auspiciousness, the life-everlasting and knowledge-unlimited, we have to "look within." It is "within" us. In this context, the following 'Song of the Soul' which is a classic will be read with interest :

Unattached am I; of nature Eternal Existence-
Knowledge-Bliss am I;
I am, ***that*** *am I, which is the irreducible,*
immortal, endless Factor.
Eternal, ever pure, ever liberated am I,
Formlessness my only form; of nature I am an
all-pervading, homogeneous mass of "BLISS."
I am, that am I, which is the irreducible,
immortal, endless Factor.
Eternal, boundless, formless, I am of nature
Pure Light and I revel in my own self.
I am the Peace that lies beyond Nature,
I am of nature ever—abiding "Bliss"—
I am, that am I, which is the irreducible,
immortal, endless Factor.
I am the Supreme Truth that lies beyond all truths,
of Delusion, I am the Supreme Light;
I am, that am I, which is the irreducible,
immortal, endless Factor.
I am different from the multiple names and forms;
Pure knowledge alone is my form; I am the
imperishable;
I am of nature joyous;
I am, that am I, which is the irreducible,
immortal, endless Factor.
I am of the form of Inner Ruler, anvil-like changeless;
And all-pervading; I am in my real nature (none
other than) the Supreme Self;

*I am, that am I, which is the irreducible,
immortal, endless Factor.*
I am of nature a Witness of all the pairs of opposites;
Motionless, most ancient, in my form I am the Eternal Witness of everything;
*I am, that am I, which is the irreducible,
immortal, eternal Factor.*
I am a mass of Consciousness; I am a mass of Knowledge too;
I am (ever) a non-doer; I am non-enjoyer.
*I am, that am I, which is the irreducible,
immortal, endless Factor.*
I am my Real Nature, I need no other foundation or support or sub-stratum, but at once I am in my Real Nature
The Foundation or support or substratum for all things and beings.
I am of Nature self-contented, self-sufficient in that I have in me all my desires fulfilled.
*I am, that am I, which is the irreducible,
immortal, endless Factor.*
Through knowledge and repeated discrimination one comes to realise that one is but a witness;
Such a one, established in the "I am witness consciousness"
Is the liberated sage.
Pots, cups, saucers are all in essence nothing but the mud in which they have been shaped.
So too the entire world of phenomenal objects is nothing but the Supreme Truth.
So roars our Divine Knowledge.

❑❑

20

WHAT ARE WE WAITING FOR?

"Thought takes man out of servitude into freedom".
— **Emerson**

SECRET OF SELF-LIBERATION

I have the highest admiration for Dale Carnegie. He was probably the first man among those outside the Church in a long time to remind us through his book, *How to win Friends and Influence People* to think of the other man's feelings instead of one's own. Excellent precept which he reinforced with a number of examples. But the trouble is, he did not go far enough for the simple reason that he put expediency before principles and religious principles in particular. I believe he must have sensed this himself. Because, he brought out a second book with a different background which bore the down-to-earth title *How to Stop Worrying and Start Living* which normally could have been called "The quest for the Peace that Passeth Understanding" or something like that. Having stuck to purely secular approach in his earlier work, he might have recoiled from creating an impression that he had turned religious overnight. Maybe his return to religion was not spectacular. But all the same it is there for everyone to see and bear witness. He has talked of doing good without expectation of gratefulness — which is solid philosophy. He has exhorted us to pray. Is that not practical religion? I cannot recall having read anything of this sort in his earlier work.

But again I am forced to join issue on one of his surmises in *How to Stop Worrying*. Dale Carnegie quotes Stephen Leacock:

> *"How strange it is, our little procession of life! The child says, 'When I am a big boy.' But what is that? The big boy says 'When I grow up.' And then when grown up, he says, 'When I get married.' But to be married, what is that after all? The thought changes to 'When I am able to retire.' And then, when retirement comes, he likes back over the landscape traversed; a cold wind seems to sweep over it; somehow he has missed it all, and it is gone......"*

and concludes that we are perpetually putting off living and asks pathetically, "What are we waiting for?" My point is that the school boy's anxiety to grow out of his school, a toiler looking forward to his retirement and so on, do not mean that they are not living in the present. On a more earthly level I feel that we are not bothered about the present for the simple reason that we are right in the midst of it. We know what we have on hand. It is the thought of the morrow which is still unhatched that inspires hope or injects gloom into a man's bosom. He has power (if only he would realise it) to mould the future and attain what he has failed to achieve so far in his life; or repeat the success he has tasted earlier or is probably enjoying at present. We can recall the wise words of Barnie Baruch, who had the rare distinction of being adviser to a succession of American Presidents:

> *"I have known, as who has not, personal disappointments and despair. But always the thought of tomorrow has buoyed me up. I have looked to the future all my life. I still do. I still believe that with courage and intelligence we can make the future bright with fulfilment."*

THE DRIVING FORCE

The driving force which propels men to look to the future, is not, I repeat, mere postponement of living. It is the quest, that eternal (if unconscious) quest, for freedom. The school boy who smarts at the restrictive discipline of school education hopes he would be free once he leaves his studies. The unmarried man looks forward to married life because he feels that it will bring him greater freedom as the undisputed head of his family, that benevolent autocrat. The man in his prime eagerly looks forward to retirement as he hopes, nay fondly believes, that he will be free from the necessity of drudging for a living or conforming to the conventions of a working life. We have achieved a five-day weak because we wanted to be free during the weekends. We hear of so many freedoms: political freedom, freedom from fear, hunger, poverty, illiteracy, freedom for worship. Who has not heard of the famous Four Freedoms of F.D.R.? Have not the poet and philosopher called death the freedom of the soul, its release from its prison which is this physical body?

"Will this thirst for freedom
Be ever quenched?"

Wails one oriental poet. Even the behaviour of the youngster playing truant, married men and women seeking pleasure outside marriage, defying legal or religious scruples, are all often symbolic expressions of the urge to assert one's freedom. Thus the quest for freedom goes on and on, but, alas the freedom so much sought after evaporates the moment we enter the state which was supposed to usher it in.

It is worthwhile pondering over this tantalizing concept of elusive freedom. Freedom is freedom in a given situation and is therefore relative. To a prisoner, freedom means getting out of prison, but does it convey the same to a man out of prison?

Eternal Spirit of the chainless Mind.
Brightest in dungeons, Liberty! thou art,
For there thy habitation is the heart-
The heart which love of Thee alone can bind.

— Byron—The Prisoner of Chillon

To a subject nation, freedom means absence of foreign domination, but to a free country it is merely a concept which does not apply *to them*. Those who have almost all the freedoms, why do they still not feel free? As in the case of happiness, we are not likely to seize real freedom from any external agency as it is in our minds or it is nowhere. The poet's sublime intuition many times blossoms into the highest philosophical truth as can be seen from the following:

Stone walls do not a prison make,
Nor iron bars a cage,
Minds innocent and quiet take
That for an hermitage;
If I have freedom in my love
And in my soul am free
Angels alone, that soar above,
Enjoy such liberty.

— Lovelace, *To Althea from Prison*

My mind to me a kingdom is;
Such present joys therein I find
That it excels all other bliss
That earth affords or grows by kind;
Though much I want which most would have
Yet still my mind forbids to crave

—Edward Dyer,
My Mind to Me a Kingdom is

But it must be conceded that the orientals, particularly the ancient Hindus, scored over followers of other religions in getting to the core of the problem. For them liberation is the summum bonum of all existence. It is the breaking of all shackles which bind human minds and not what restricts his person. When we realize the true nature of our soul, which is eternally free, but which the mind feels by delusion to be always bound; when we realize in meditation that we are souls, part of the Universal Soul that pervades everything, whose true nature is unconditioned joy, pure consciousness and existence absolute, we are free, we are truly liberated. We have to meditate constantly on this concept, assert our freedom and feel free.

SIMILARITY IN EXPRESSION

There is a striking similarity in the expressions of mystics of different countries and religions who have pierced the veil and perceived the oneness of all existence. Their brotherhood is unique. Their unanimity is unquestioned. Their outlook has a uniformity that has sprung up spontaneously. Is it not a sign of the essential oneness of humanity that whenever a great religious leader made his appearance anywhere, his sway over the masses had been more massive than that of kings and conquerors, dictators and despots? You might have beard of Sankaracharya (meaning Sankara, the teacher), the intellectual and mystic giant who strode across the vast sub-continent of India in the seventh century like a colossus. His conquest of the mind of his countrymen put to shame the military victory of the mightiest of political conquerors, past and present. What was the secret of his supreme power? He declared and proved in the most scientific manner that 'the Godhead alone is real, the phenomenal world is relatively unreal, the individual soul is nothing but the Universal Soul.' Scientific? Yes. Because he exhorted that no postulate should be acceptable to anyone which did not stand the test of rigid and remorseless reasoning. He was the greatest of conquerors of the spirit by the spirit. A conquest which liberates unlike military conquest which enslaves. There had been only one equal to him — Jesus Christ. Did Christ envisage a military conquest of the world for upholding the tenets of Christianity? As a matter of fact, did he ever proclaim himself as the founder of a religion bearing his name? Yet the followers of Sankaracharya and Christ embraced Hinduism and Christianity and rejected these two great teachers*

If instead of being a binding, uniting force, an uplifting faith, a source of true freedom, peace and joy, of the brotherhood of man and oneness of all sentient and insentient life, religion has left man uninhibited in perpetrating and perpetuating all sorts of follies, and the worst of all follies, war, it is not the mistake of religion. Nor is it correct to blame science or the scientist for our lack of

---

*The allusion here is to the famous statement by Louis Fischer on Gandhi — that he embraced Christ but rejected Christianity.

humanity. They are mere platitudes. Because, in the words of George Bernard Shaw:

> *"Science and religion at loggerheads are reflected politically in a suicidal world war. The popular nation that one of the two must be all right and the other all wrong is not reasoning at all, but thoughtless, unobservant jumping at conclusions. ....If we could get them entirely right, the contradictions between them would disappear. We should have a religious science and a scientific religion in a single synthesis."*

❑❑

21

CATCH THEM YOUNG

"Oh, that thou hadst hearkened to My Commandments! Then had thy peace been as a river."

— Isaiah 48:18

NURSING THE YOUTHFUL MINDS

The other day I was shocked to see a sixteen year old boy read in a dull and lifeless manner that beautiful picture of "A True Gentleman" by Cardinal Newman. To this teenager it did not mean anything more than an ordinary literary piece to be read for being able to answer a possible question in his examination. I remember distinctly how elevated I felt when first I read an extract of the same piece in the front page of a diary when *I* was a teenager. That picture made an indelible impression on my youthful mind. I cut it and pasted it in my collection of inspirational material. I have read it a number of times and almost learnt it by heart. I would like to believe that I have profited by it. Apart from profiting, I am the richer in being able to appreciate its excellence, both in style and content. I felt pity for the boy and probably his generation which, it appears, has not so much use for idealism as the one to which I belonged. A friend of mine to whom I confided, reassured me saying that to a boy who evinces keen interest in the study of science (which was the case with this boy), any other subject fails to exercise fascination! Frankly, it left me feeling no better. When this boy was quite young I had tried to instil in him some idealism, but in the atmosphere prevailing probably in *his* circle, what little he might have absorbed must have evaporated!

I have heard it said that gratefulness does not come just naturally to children, that it has to be planted in their minds and nurtured. Could the same not be said of almost all the noble sentiments that find a place in human breast? The sublimity of truthfulness, the glory of self-sacrifice, the warmth of compassion, are all themes which have to be pondered over, and fixed firmly in our consciousness if we are to expose ourselves to their humanising influence.

Present-day education sadly neglects the opportunity of winning over youthful minds to the ways of gracious and idealistic living. Nay, it would appear that we are once for all banishing noble sentiments from the lives of coming generations by not taking the initiative in these matters. This passivity, this indifference in instructing the young in matters of the heart and spirit is the greatest dereliction of duty we are culpable of and amounts to a betrayal of the trust reposed in us by our ancestors. We are not handing the torch down. As Edmund Burke has said.

> *"All that is necessary for the triumph of evil is that good men do nothing."*

We have tacitly been instrumental in handing over the moral and religious instruction of the young to the TV programmes and films. No wonder film stars and cowboys have become the heroes of the younger generation.

Elsewhere in this volume reference has been made to Joseph Addison's famous essay on the 'Pleasures of Imagination.' He was dwelling on the pleasure one can eke out by day-dreaming scenic beauty as a pastime. Those of us who are yet capable of a few thrills by recapturing the heroic deeds of Christ who could send out a prayer for his executioners saying. "Father, forgive them. For they know not what they do", or the great sacrifice of Gautama the Buddha, who stole away from his palace at dead of night, renouncing his kingdom, comfort, wife and the infant at her breast, in search of a cure for human suffering — how dare we deny such thrills to our sons and daughters? We are robbing them of a precious heritage.

Frankly, I have no idea of how my Western adult friends spend the time between their return from work and the next morning. If it is true that a good number of them are away from homes attending parties, eating out in public restaurants and hotels or watching film shows or plays, or getting a kickout of indulging in drinks and witnessing naughty night-club cabaret, I should think that it is the greatest single tragedy since the crucifixation of Christ or the assassination of Abe Lincoln. We are throwing away the most precious opportunity to be ourselves within the secure walls of our homes, watching our children grow into sturdy manhood or womanhood, strengthening our character and thus our children's. Let us go back to the ways of life of our more sober and, incidentally, more happy, ancestors. I do not mean that we should put the clock back. Where we have burnt the boats, go back we cannot. But where we can, why should we not? Let us spend our evenings in the company of our children, telling them the glowing tales of heroism which bring out the beauty of loftier sentiments, emotions and ways of life.

We have all heard of the slogan in sports and athletics: "Catch them Young!" Sports talents should be detected early and training given when the enthusiast is quite young. Where there is no innate or inborn talent, practice, constant, regular practice, will largely make up for lack of natural aptitude. Similarly, we must inculcate the religious spirit in our children when they are quite young. Religion must be fed along with mother's milk — that is, from infancy. We cannot just leave a child to learn from experience that fire will burn. In the same way, religion cannot wait to be learnt and practised by children till they know from their own experience what it is all about. A child sometimes refuses food. It has to be coaxed or forced to take it. In the same way, a child should be taught, even when there is no natural inclination, to have a wholesome fear of God and simple moral laws. It will thank you in later life for having taught it. Our children are our stern judges, too. If we fail them, they will curse and despise us when it would be too late to do anything about it.

Alongside we must teach them politeness and good manners - those small acts of self-sacrifice meant to please others and lubricate the wheels of day-to-day living. We should set example ourselves. If example does not bring forth emulation, use gentle force, use your persuasive powers. Cajole them, coax them if you can, and threaten and punish or ridicule if you must. There is no escape from duty either for you or for the young ones.

THE CHILDREN HAVE TO BE DISCIPLINED

We are living in a world of psychology. Nowadays anything passes for psychology. New words and phrases like repression, fixation and self-expression are bandied about by all and sundry. It is but common sense that we cannot allow our kids, not even ourselves, to indulge in all our fancies. Children have to be disciplined, but it need not be a fierce or thoughtless process. You can do that in an enlightened manner. That is where you can prove your mettle. It is a test for you, you cannot shirk. All of us cannot hope to see our children blossoming into Florence Nightingales or Abe Lincolns. Nor is it necessary either. Still we must see that they take their place as enlightened, law-abiding citizens, happy and relaxed themselves, useful to others, their society, their country and thereby their world — through religion. If we can achieve this, it will be no small achievement. That will be *our* individual contribution to the welfare of the world.

❑❑

22

DIFFERENT METHODS OF APPROACH TO GOD

"Lead me from the unreal to the Real
Lead me from darkness to light,
Lead me from death to Immortality."

— **Upanishads**

HUMAN NATURE IS ESSENTIALLY THE SAME EVERYWHERE

But each individual reacts differently to different stimuli. For example, if a man has gone through great suffering and arrived at a stage of comparative ease and happiness, his attitude to the suffering of other people can be either of the two entirely opposite ones: (a) He might like to see that others are not put to suffering needlessly or avoidably, and be prompted to take measures in that direction. There are many examples in history of erstwhile sufferers having turned out to be great benefactors of mankind. The life of Hellen Keller is a shining and unforgettable example of a handicapped individual blazing a glorious trail to help the rehabilitation of fellow sufferers condemned to a dark existence, or one which is robbed of the pleasures of verbal communication with others. (b) Or the sufferer of the past turns a cynic and would derive a morbid satisfaction when others have to go through similar tribulations. The case of victimised daughter-in-law developing into a cruel mother-in-law is too well known to need elaboration. Not that there is no third category of the middle-of-the-road, indifferent onlooker who just does not care to reflect on the afflictions of others. That is, there is no reaction and if it is an enlightened indifference, it cannot be wholly indefensible. In any case, we have seen that reaction to a stimulus varies. But for this fact, psychology would not have been such a complicated, and sometimes misleading, science!

Then there is the question of temperaments. For some known or unknown reasons (assuming that at the start of the race handicaps were equal to all contenders), human beings are of different temperaments or natures. In one, muscular strength is predominant and the individual so endowed engages himself in ceaseless activity propelled by an accretion of excessive physical energy. Another type is predominantly emotional, moved by occurences, prone to be attached or devoted, longing to love and pining to be loved. A third category consists of the predominantly intellectual. He wants to put everything to the proof and will accept any theory or fact only on being convinced by reasoning. Thus three main types emerge: the man of muscle, the man of heart and the man of head. Mark the word 'predominantly' in this context. For, no man is exclusively classifiable under any of these - he is a combination of any two or all the three.

Religion has differently been defined by thinkers. "Religion deals with essential mystery which, in the last analysis, no human language can fully clothe or communicate. Religion is participation in the mystery," says one great philosopher. But the common man of all ages has been a novice, uninitiated into the realm of intellectual, didactic or dialectic disquisition. Understandably so, because philosophy if indulged from a purely academic angle, divorced from practical life and religion, assumes a lofty, exalted air of the uncommon and probably, of the understandable. The common man, instinctively associates religion with God. For one, unsophisticated, God is essentially anthropomorphic. He imagines a God with from because he cannot grasp the concept of the formless. Some religions (and they are among the most ancient) provide the believer definite ideas about that anthropomorphic concept through the medium of divine incarnations. For example, the Hindus, whose religion is among the oldest known to man, are at liberty to adopt their 'Ishta Devata' which means 'the preferred deity,' a divine incarnation selected by oneself to suit one's own taste or inclination. The learned man, the real knower, does not scoff at such a choice because he know that it provides the best scope for that form of worship known as devotion or adoration that helps man to go all out in his surrender to God through love. As a matter of fact, any one in his intellectual arrogance deriding the simple man's act of devotion to, and worship of, his chosen deity is sternly reprimanded. This idea is so poignantly brought out in the *Shepherd's Prayer* by Jalaluddin Rumi.*

Without premeditation I have taken up the 'path of love' first for discussion and that itself is testimony to its pre-eminence among the different approaches to God and Godliness. It is because the inordinate, if inarticulate longing to love and be loved is the lot of most humans. The void resulting from non-fulfilment of man's most elementary, but imperious need - to love and be loved–has been the subject of research of many pioneering modern psychologists. But man of even earlier ages, the soundness of whose judgement is not so lightly to be dismissed, intuitively guessed the whole range and ramifications of human emotions. Earthly love is but earthy. Selfish love can never satisfy. Possessive love cannot endure. Blind love of the erotic type seemingly can, but really can never, ennoble, elevate. The reason is not far to seek. For all human love, whether it be the mother's or the lover's is tainted with selfishness and exacts of its object its pound of flesh. All love, as the old English writer, Robert Burton, long ago said, is a kind of slavery. If the mother's love has been the sublime subject of many a poet's muse, it is because it comes nearest to pure love. What does that mean, 'Pure love'? Love, like any other emotion, is purified when there is no expectation of return or fear of rejection. Of pure love it has been said:

---

* See Appendix

"Love by its very nature is renunciation; It cannot be made to fulfil selfish desires."

Love of one human being for another, in whichever from or relationship it exists, is bound to founder or flounder at one stage or other. It leaves one aching for a more satisfying and satisfactory love. How exactly does a mother feel when she sees her beloved son being claimed by a comparative stranger, in the form of his sweetheart, as her own? Who, other than God, can be the object of pure, satisfying, elevating love? Has it not been declared that 'God is love'? The love of God stands on a unique footing and there is nothing parallel to it.

A LOVER OF GOD

Let me give here a piece of the outpourings of the heart of a *lover of God*. See how his language flows alongside his love. Actually, is not love of God a perennial river flowing into the Ocean of Love, God Himself? When the river approaches the ocean, all its turbulence, all its wantonness, vandalism, playfulness are calmed down. What sediment or silt it has collected is unceremoniously shed. Once it enters the ocean joyously, it loses its separate identity and merges with the vast expanse of water. Similarly, the lover of God becomes purer, nobler, more peaceful and more joyous as he gets closer to God through love for Him. Now to come back, read a section of *The Imitation of Christ* of Thomas A Kempis who is no stranger to the reader:

"Oh, Lord God, my holy Lover! when Thou comest to my heart, all that is within me shall exult with joy..... A great thing is love, a great good every way; which alone lightens every burden and bears equally every inequality. For it carries a burden without being burdened, and makes every bitter thing sweet and savoury. The noble love of Jesus impels a man to do great things, and ever excites him to desire that which is more perfect. Love wills to be on high, and refuses to be held back by things

below. Love wills to be free and to be detached from all worldly affection, so that its inward vision be not hindered, and that it suffer no entanglement in temporal prosperity, or discomfiture of misfortune. Nothing is sweeter than love, nothing stronger, nothing higher, nothing wiser, nothing more pleasant, nothing fuller or better in heaven or on earth; for love is born of God, and cannot rest but in God, above all created things...... Love is swift, sincere, devoted, cheerful, and delightful; strong, patient, faithful, prudent, long suffering, manly and NEVER SELF-SEEKING. ***For when a man seeks himself, he falls from love."***

It is quite clear that the love of the devotee for God is a self-abnegating love, it liberates instead of enslaving unlike ordinary human love.

Love of God need not conform to any set specification. There can be variety and richness. It can be colourfully sublime and imaginatively improvised. God can be loved in different relationships. In one the devotee imagines himself to be the servant and God the master; or he may take up the attitude of a parent and adore God with the solicitude of a mother for her child. A third variation is that of the relationshiop of a friend — love of one to a friend, on equal footing. Or God is the sweetheart and the soul pines in love due to separation and longs to be united to the Beloved. The intensity of love drives the devotee mad and he is obsessed day and night with only one thing — love for the Lord.

In a world torn by strife and hatred, the supremacy of the Path of Love as a sovereign remedy for its ills should be self-evident. Not only for liberation, but even for worldly existence, unselfish love is unquestionably the golden means. There is no doubt that love triumphs over hatred and evil.*

---

* Truly to love ourselves we must love God,-
To love God we must all his creatures love,-
To love his creatures, both ourselves and Him,
This love is all that's wise, fair good and happy!

—Philip James Bailey

Next we shall deal with the man of muscle, the man of action. How can he attain to God? Through *selfless* performance of all action, believing work to be worship, consecrating all deeds by dedicating their results to God. Note the point of convergence between the Path of Love and the Path of Action. Through love the devotee constantly remembers God. We have already covered good ground in three of the previous chapters entitled "Work, the Emancipator" which should enable us to appreciate the idea underlying the Path of Action.

The third path, the Path of Knowledge is for the thinker, the contemplative. In him the head, the intellect predominates. He has realised the futility of worldly knowledge and worldly life and bends his will and energy to the Godward ascent through enquiry and discrimination—discrimination between the real and the unreal, between the permanent and the transitory.* By analysis and reasoning, with the help of the Scriptures, he arrives at the unshakable conviction that God alone (in his impersonal, formless aspect, the immanent and transcendent) is real and all else unreal, and also the individual soul is nothing but a part of that Oversoul.

That words real and unreal are to be understood in their correct meaning. If I tell you that the world is unreal, it will not carry conviction. It is unreal because everything in it undergoes change and passes off the stage after its part is played. If you met a child of today after twenty years, you cannot recognize him. The youth of today becomes a tottering, old man with the passage of time. Then comes death. While everything changes, life as such goes on. The Stage Manager, the Playwright alone remains. Conceding that the state of enlightenment does exist different from, and superior to, our common existence, the two can be compared to the waking and dreaming state of our day-to-day life. What appears to a dreamer to be so realistic while asleep becomes unreal and shadowlike to him when awake. Similarly, what is real and solid to our normal perception is unreal to the realized soul.*

---

* See Appendix *C*.

The Path of knowledge is no doubt superior to the other two paths, but it is also the most difficult of the three, because knowledge is not mere intellectual conviction. It is realization. He who 'knows' becomes. He then does not exist apart from the Supreme and becomes a *'jivan-mukta'*, a man who has attained salvation in this very life.

Then there is the phenomenon of Grace. It is not easily defined and grasping the idea is still more difficult. Irrespective of the stage of evolution of a soul, there is possible the over-powering intervention of Divine Grace which cuts asunder the knots of one's heart and catapults it to that supreme state — liberation. It is as spontaneous as it is instantaneous, inexplicable yet possible.

We have referred to in an earlier chapter the sudden transformation of an individual deeply inured to worldly life — the life in the flesh. As a flash of lightning, the futility of the secular life dawns on him and thereafter his life has nothing to do with existence at mundane level. He turns an ascetic, a lover of God or a real knower of God. Some chance happening, a stray remark, some wild adventure forms the immediate cause and rents the veil of ignorance and the man is at that moment reborn as a saint. There can be two real causes (as distinct from the immediate cause) for this sudden fruition or fulfilment of evolution. One, the inexplicable divine intervention, Grace. Second, there is nothing left for retribution, as merit and demerit balance and thus he becomes free.

---

*In this connection, it would be pertinent to refer to the 'concept of illusion,' the famous 'Maya' theory. The scientific basis of this concept may be explained thus :

> *"For example, the modern scientist carried in his head two sets of ideas about the world. The simpler set deals with large scale objects — you, me, tables, chairs, rocks etc. For these the scientist like any other man, has workaday ideas about solidity, location, reality. But when the scientist forces his thinking down to basic levels, a new and abstract set of ideas comes into play. A table, viewed with the precise tools of the atomic physicist, is a shadowy, whirling set of vague and elusive electric charges. So viewed, the table completely loses its large scale illusion of solidity."*
>
> **—Warren Weaver**

Here again there is the parallel of a bank account. Can a bank have account for a client with neither debit nor credit balance? Either the bank owes him when he has some money left to his credit. Or the Bank has lent money to the customer for a consideration - interest. When a bank does not owe anything to the client nor he to the bank, what happens? The account is simply closed!

Now in the case of merit and demerit too, the above contingency does arise in regard to an individual life and the operation of the Law of Resultant Action. If a man has sinned, he has to suffer for it. For good deeds, too, he has to enjoy the reward till the merit is exhausted. This is not confined to a single life span.* The theory of rebirth or reincarnation, which has come to be accepted almost universally as one founded on scientific or natural postulates, spreads the cycle of accumulation-exhaustion (of merit or demerit) to subsequent embodiment or birth. If, in the evolution of a soul, at any moment, the two (merit and demerit) balance coincidentally with God-realization, there is no more reincarnation or rebirth for it. There is only absorption into the Supreme. Such absorption into the Supreme or supreme absorption should not be taken to mark the termination of life, physical death. As a matter of fact, the word 'jivan-mukta' (literally, the one liberated while yet alive or in this very life,) itself connotes that the supreme moment comes while living. The absorption is irrevocable, there can be no going back either voluntary or involuntary. And why should there be, because it is the summum bonum, the raison d'etre of the soul's effort? The journey of the soul has come to an end — it has reached its haven and home. The case of real saints turning back on

---

* Life is the transmigration of a soul Through various bodies, various states of being; New manners, passions, new pursuits in each; In nothing, save in Consciousness, the same.
Infancy, adolescence, manhood, age, Are always moving onward, always losing Themselves in one another, lost at length Like undulations on the strand of death.

— James Montgomery (1771–1854)
— Life

God and re-entering the stage as worldly men is unheard of. Where we do have a seeming exception, it must be assumed that the 'saint' had indeed been a charlatan, a counterfeit and not a genuine one. As a flower falls off when the fruit from it has emerged, the body of the realized man falls off in due time. The soul merges into the Supreme at the death of the physical body and thus there is no need for a rebirth.

We shall give here an analogy to illustrate the above final absorption and shedding of the physical body. A vessel containing water is reflecting the sun's rays in the form of a patch of bright light on a nearby wall. There are two factors—the sun or sun-light and its reflection. The water in the vessel is dashed to the ground and is absorbed by it. What has happened to the reflection? Has it not merged with the original beam of light ? The Oversoul reflects through the mediums of the physical body. The reflection is the individual soul. When the physical body returns to its elements, the individual soul merges with the Oversoul.

❑❑

23

THREE STORIES

"There is no supernatural, there is only God's great natural. There is no miracle; there is only the ever-present possibility of laying hold on divine law on higher and higher levels of using it."

— Eric Butterworth — *Life is for Living*

THE PHENOMENON OF WORLDLY MEN

In the last chapter we referred to the phenomenon of worldly men transformed at a critical moment in their destiny into saints by a casual remark of another in their circle or an unforeseen incident or a wild adventure, to mention only a few of the apparent or immediate causes. I shall now narrate three stories by way of illustration, stripped of their native trimmings. Whether they are truly historical or merely fictitious does not materially alter the validity of the illustrations. In ancient Hindu literature, there is generally an exuberance of occurences or statements which are often super-natural or hyper-miraculous: angels and men communicating with one another, God descending on earth taking various forms, even subhuman ones, to save His devotees, His setting at nought 'natural' laws and so on. It requires a particular conditioning to be able to read them without wincing! I am an incurable optimist and find unmistakable signs of the modern man hesitating to dismiss everything which he cannot grasp with his not unlimited intelligence as fictitious. As evidence, see what Eric Butterworth has said (quoted above).

Now to my story-telling. First we shall take the story of Valmiki, the great sage-author of the Hindu epic, *Ramayana*. He was in his youth a highway robber, who lived on the outskirts of a forest. To maintain his wife, children and himself, he used to way-lay unwary travellers and relieve them of their valuables. Where there was resistance, he used violence. He must have lived like that for number of years.

To his great good fortune, one day a group of sages was passing through his haunts. True to his calling, he halted them under threats and asked them to surrender their all. He must have been desperate, or his destiny must have beckoned him. Otherwise couldn't he have seen that the sages could have nothing of use to him except perhaps their water jugs?

The sages too were rather in a mood to humour him. Or they had come on purpose to reform him visualizing his brilliant future. They agreed to surrender all their possessions on one condition: That he would go to his wife and children while they waited, and ascertained from them if they would share his sins which he was perpetrating for their maintenance. The robber was surprised. He was sure they would. Yet, strangely, he retired immediately to his hut and confronted them with the question. Contrary to his expectation, they repudiated they had any share in his sins. He was bound to support them; if he had chosen to take to banditry, it was not at their behest — so they argued. The necessary shock thus administered, he returned to the waiting sages, fell at their feet and begged to be shown the way for his redemption. Initiating him to penance by way of expiation, they departed. After a lapse of some months or years, they came back and were delighted to see the former bandit transfixed to the ground, chanting the divine name. Ant hills surrounded the new sage and connecting this to his transformation, they christened him 'Valmiki' — *Valmika* meaning ant hill.

CHARM OF AN ORIGINAL WORK

The second is the story of Tulsidas, the great Hindi poet and saint, who translated the *Ramayana* into his language, retaining all the charm of an original work as if he had written it himself on inspiration. Tulsi was a young man, full of zest for life. He was married early to a dazzling beauty, whose charm rendered him her slave. He could not suffer separation from her even for a while. Once she happened to be in her parent's home without him. Goaded by his infatuation, he hurried thither. He braved rough weather and swam across a swollen river late at night. When at last he reached her house, every one was asleep. Ashamed of gate-crashing at that late hour, he scaled the walls of her house, tugging at a python which he mistook for a sturdy creeper. When his wife woke up and saw him blood-stained and shabby, she chided him for his blind infatuation for her and casually remarked that if only he had directed a fraction of such devotion to God, he would have secured his salvation. That was the signal for the spiritual awakening of Tulsidas who was that instant transformed into a great devotee of God.

The third story, that of the musician-saint of South India, Purandara Dasa, has more than a small element of the dramatic about it. He was originally a jeweller-cum-money-lender. He was an abject miser, to part with money was to him equivalent to parting with life itself! He was rich enough, still his miserliness reduced him to the state of a money-mulcting-machine.

The time was fast approaching for his enlightenment. A poor priest came to him one day seeking monetary assistance for a religious function in his house. The miser, seated in his business premises, turned the priest out with abuses. The priest, undaunted, went to the residence of Dasa at the rear and begged Dasa's wife for a donation. Conscious of her husband's attitude towards money and yet not desiring to send away the poor man empty handed, she took out her costly nose-screw, set with precious stones which she could legitimately claim as her own, being a present of her parents, and gifted it to the suppliant.

The priest, pleased yet wanting to tease, offered the ornament to Dasa himself for sale. His suspicions aroused, Dasa locked the thing securely in a safe, and rushed to his wife demanding an explanation. The desperate lady decided to end her life by taking poison. While she raised the cup with the fatal drink to her lips, something fell into it from nowhere. To her great astonishment, she found it to be her nose-screw which she dutifully handed over to her husband. Flabbergasted, Dasa dashed back to his shop and on unlocking the safe, found the jewel kept in it missing. The poor priest had also vanished.

At this dramatic turn of events, scales fell off the eyes of the miser who renounced his wealth then and there and chose the life of a wandering minstrel, worshipping God through music.

❑❑

24

HERE AND HEREAFTER

......Who would fardels bear,

To grunt and sweat under a weary life; But that the dread of something after death-The undiscovered country, from whose bourn No traveller returns, - puzzles the will; And makes us rather bear those ills we have, Than fly to others that we know not of?

— William Shakespeare, *Hamlet*

THE FEAR OF DEATH

Death draws the curtain finally and man leaves this stage at the appointed time. The reason for most human beings living in fear of death can be traced to this abrupt end and the mystery that surrounds his state thereafter. What happens to man or his soul after he shuffles off his mortal coil? Does he live this life for its own sake? Has it any purpose or aim? Is there a life beyond? Does he come to live on this earth again by being born afresh? Does humanity move towards a brighter future? These are some of the questions that have baffled mankind. Many theories have been propounded — concoctions of conjectures and surmises based on what little it is given to mortals to perceive ever so dimly.

To try to go into a detailed discussion of even one of the questions is clearly beyond the scope of this little volume. All I propose to do here is to give relevant quotations from various sources and authorities and leave the reader to draw what conclusions he will.

"I am the resurection, saith the Lord; he that believeth in me though he were dead, yet shall

he live; and whosoever liveth and believeth in me, shall never die."

—The Bible

"It is in dying that we are born to everlasting life."

— St. Francis of Assissi

"Just as men cast off worn out garments and put on new ones, the soul casts off worn out bodies and takes on new ones.

— The Bhagavat Gita

"A Man is not completely born until he is dead. Why then should we grieve that a new child is born among the immortals? We are spirits. That bodies should be lent us, while they can afford us pleasure, assist us in acquiring knowledge or in doing good to our fellow creatures, is a kind and benevolent act of God. When they become unfit for these purposes and afford us pain instead of pleasure, instead of an aid become an encumbrance, it is equally kind and benevolent that a way is provided by which we may get rid of them. Death is that way.

Our friend and we were invited abroad on a party of pleasure which is to last forever. His chair was ready first and he is gone before us. We could not all conveniently start together; and why should you and I be grieved at this, since we are soon to follow and know where to find him?"

— Benjamin Franklin

"Many people seem to feel that science has some how made 'religious ideas' untimely and old-fashioned. But I think science has a real surprise for the skeptics. Science, for instance, tells that nothing in nature, not even the tiniest particle, can disappear without a trace. Nature does not know extinction. All it knows is transformation. Now, if God applies this fundamental principle to the most minute and insignificant parts of His universe, doesn't it make sense to assume that

He applies it also to the human soul? Everything science has taught me - and continues to teach me - strengthens my belief in the continuity of our spiritual existence after death. Nothing disappears without a trace."

— Dr. Wernher Von Braun, Space Physicist

"Clearly, God's answer to death is life. In fact, the Bible preaches a faith based on life, not death. It tells us that what appears to be death only seems so, that the real fact is life eternal."

— Dr. Norman Vincent Peale

"We, alas, in this materialistic age, obsessed by the pursuit of pleasure, forget that mere enjoyment is not the be-all and end-all of existence. If we accept God and our own immortality we under-stand that our lives are not meant to be a joy ride but a time — all too short — of preparation; a moment, in terms of eternity, of testing and endurance, when we stand poised upon the threshold of the hereafter."

— Dr. A.J. Cronin

"It has taken millions of years to bring us to our present state, and it may take long, long periods before we evolve into our full stature. But He has placed the capabilities within us. The grand design, which is sometimes hard to discern, and the upward urge, which is sometimes slow to act, are His great gifts to us."

— Dr. Warren Weaver

❑❑

25

HOPE FOR ALL

The illusion that times that were are better than those that are have probably pervaded all ages.

— Horace Greeley

(Is humanity progressing, or is human society disintegrating? Do all the technological, scientific and social advances mean a better, more integrated human being, at peace with himself, his surroundings and his fellow creatures, or is he developing into a monster? This question, asked at periodic intervals throughout human history, is likely to depress a thinking man if he does not view history in proper perspective and arrive at a balanced judgement. Man is a unique being in that, whereas in all non-human life, might prevails and the struggle for existence is a grim reality, he alone has organised his society in such a manner that not only are the weak freed from fear of the mighty, but actually afforded all protection to live their life as peacefully as anyone else as a matter of right. The following symposium published by the author some years ago in an Indian journal remains as topical today as it was when it appeared for the first time.)

Question: I have often heard old uncle speak nostalgically of the good old days and asserting that the world is heading towards ruin as there is all round deterioration in values. How far is he correct?

Answer: I don't think there is much truth in such a sweeping assertion. Probably, in his youth he found more objects of pleasure around him which no longer delight his senses. Therefore he feels that the world of those days was a better place to live in.

If you take a detached view, you will notice such tremendous progress, not only technologically, but even on the moral plane taking place. Let me warn you that morality is not something which relates to the relations between the sexes alone. As a matter of fact, I am referring to morality in spheres other than sex!

Question: Well done, we shall for the time being leave alone the 'tangled thickets of sex.' Followers of certain religions call this the 'Iron Age' in which there will be progressive deterioration of righteousness and in the end there will be a deluge and total effacement of life on this planet.

Answer: It cannot be established that men and woman of the present age are more wicked because we read in our classics and epics that people of ancient times behaved on much the same pattern. Moreover, recording of history as a true narrative of events, people and nations is of relatively recent origin. A greater part of our ancient literature is more or less imaginative writing. Since even imagination has to have some basis on facts, we conclude that there was a very flourishing civilization dating back to thousands of years.

Question: You have not answered my question regarding the cycles succeeded by a deluge.

Answer: As man's own span of life is limited, he might have imagined that the world too should have an end. We find reference to deluge in the Bible also. Even according to the Hindu cycle theory, there are still thousands of years left in the present 'Iron Age.' But if we take into account the present-day international developments, nuclear weapons and their tests, it looks the destruction of the world is, after all, not far off. All that stands between us and the total effacement of life on earth would appear to be a nuclear war.

Question: Do you mean to say that the end of the world is very near?

Answer: No, far from it. It was many years ago that the atomic weapons were discovered. The world has passed through many grave crises. We have been on the "brink" of major wars several times. There have been lesser wars in different parts of the world, but the atom bomb has been used only once, that is, in Hiroshima and Nagasaki.

Question: What guarantee is there that a major war will not break out and that the atom bomb will not be used again?

Answer: In the strictest sense, none indeed. But it would appear that the possibilities of destruction caused by nuclear weapons have been exaggerated. Before this, we had bombs with great destructive power, though of a lesser degree. There was a war when the whole world was more or less divided into warring camps. What prevented the belligerents from making the fullest use of those earlier bombs? Why was not the world bombed in every nook and corner? Moreover, human and other life has a way of adapting to all sorts of hazards, great or small.

Question: It is not clear to what you attribute the preventive deterrent.

Answer: To the instict of self-preservation. I mean the two are closely allied. We have come to realize, though not fully, that our well-being is intimately connected with other's welfare.

Question: But can America alone ward off a war by her Aid Programmes?

Answer: I never said so. What I wanted to drive home was the fact that the powers who are in possession of nuclear weapons themselves are afraid of becoming victims to them. They intend, probably, to use them more as defensive than offensive weapons. They want to speak to their opponents from a position of strength.

Question: What makes you believe that a major war will not break out?

Answer: There are several reasons. One is the gradual development of world conscience. As Jawaharlal Nehru once said, world opinion today is a major factor in international conduct. Even the wrong-doers know that their actions will not meet with the approval of at least a section of world opinion! No nation openly dare take any step which it is sure will be condemned by a majority of peoples and nations.

Question: Mere world opinion seems to be such an intangible and insubstantial thing.

Answer: Nothing could be farther from truth. World opinion takes various forms. In the present day world, the United Nations has developed into a forum for the expression of world opinion and focused it on various troubles and trouble-spots in an effort to correct the erring nation or nations. The turn the Invasion of Suez of 1956 took was major victory for world opinion.

Question: Let us come back to the original question.What makes you believe that we are not deteriorating?

Answer: The subject we were talking of, namely the U.N.O. is not unconnected to the answer to what you call your ' original question.' The existence of a world body like the U.N. has in it the seed for a better world which has so far seemed a mirage or Utopia. The fact that so many peoples of different nations, religions and races are brought together for consideration of international matters is in itself no mean achievement of human civilization. Ideas of superiority of one nation or one race or one religion are breaking down fast. Total abolition of slavery is almost within sight. Colonial expansion or subjugation and exploitation politically and economically of one nation by another is becoming a thing of the past due to the pressure of world opinion.

Question: Don't you think that people with your view are in a minority?

Answer: Certainly not. I still vividly remember the great speech of Mr. Louis St. Laurant, when he was the Canadian Prime Minister, in which he ridiculed the Western Powers who suffered from a superiority complex. He declared that the days when the 'Supermen' of Europe, sitting in their armchairs, could govern the affairs of the so-called backward nations were definitely over. But, by far, the best proof is the existence and functioning of subsidiary bodies of the U.N. like the UNESCO, WHO, the FAO etc. They have brought the peoples of the world nearer by making them co-operate with one another and share their knowledge and resources. The U.N. may well usher in the millennium by making possible the coming into existence of a World Government. National consciousness is still strong among peoples, but gradually it may give way to international consciousness. Indeed only a world Government can altogether outlaw War, the last vestige of human barbarity and brutality, by bringing about a measure of equality in the status of different peoples and removing the causes of conflict.

Question: How do you think it will affect individual lives?

Answer: When glaring inequalities in income and standard of living of individuals throughout the world are removed, when people are assured of a reasonably want-free, healthy life, it will enable individuals to devote their attention to higher pursuits and a higher life, a spiritual life. By the time the opportunity is provided, the world's millions should become alive to the need of living the higher life which can only be a spiritual life, religious life. It will need a tremendous effort. Man's wisdom can certainly make it possible and bear fruit. Humanity is definitely moving forward — there is not the least doubt about it.

❑❑

26

THE INSCRUTABILITY OF THE MEANING OF EXISTENCE

THE FINAL AIM

"Every atom in the universe is a thing complete in itself, and at the same time is only a part of a whole so vast as to be inconceivable by man. And in the same way, every individual alive today bears within him his own ends, and yet bears them so as to serve the ends of world development unknown to man.

A bee settling on a flower has stung a child. The child says the object of the bee is to sting people. A poet admires the bee sipping honey from the cup of the flower and declares that the bee lives solely in order to imbibe this nectar. A bee-keeper, observing that the bee gathers pollen and brings it to the hive, maintains that the bee's purpose is to gather honey. Another bee-keeper who has studied the life of the swarm more closely, maintains that the bee collects this honey to feed the young ones and to rear a queen, and therefore devotes itself entirely to the perpetuation of its species. A botanist notices that the bee flying with the pollen fertilizes a pistil and in this he sees the true function of the bee. Another declares that the bee lives in order to contribute to the hybridization of plants and so on.

Who is to say that we shall not go on discovering other reasons for the bee's existence? But shall we ever know what is the final and ultimate aim of the bee? The higher the human intellect rises, the more obvious it becomes that the final aim of the bee is beyond ken.

And the same is true of the final aims of historical figures and peoples and nations."

—Count Leo Tolstoy in "War and Peace."

In spite of the vast strides made by man in the fields of science and technology, the meaning of existence continues to be a mystery. Science tries hard to find *how* things happen, but does not answer the question 'why'? That is the realm of religion and philosophy. Still the mystery is not fully solved, at least not entirely satisfactorily. How often have we stood in awe at this play of life and death, birth, sustenance and dissolution! It is baffling in the extreme. The firm believer in God smiles to himself and just exclaims that it is His sport!

"Thou hast created all things and for thy pleasure they are and were created."

—Rev. 4:11.

We can only accept it for what it is. Having reconciled to it, our duty will be to play our part in this endless drama as also know the relative roles of other forms of life. Probably the simile of the relationship between an agriculturist and agriculture will enable us to get some insight.

The plant in the field is not conscious of the fact that it is part of the existence in the field and that it does not grow and exist for its own sake alone. The farmer in turn cannot view one plant individually. He prepares the ground, sows the seeds and replants them in time, arranges for the right amount of water, manure etc., to be available for the crop as a whole, thus ensuring that all the plants will have equal opportunity to grow and contribute their individual share to the harvest. Still, not all the seeds sprout, not all the plants grow equally, and it is also true that the yield from every plant is not exactly the same. Many plants wither prematurely and even when the ear of corn is ripe, not all the corn reaches the barn of the farmer. To the farmer and those who can understand farming, the operations, their timeliness, their utility and their aims are comprehensible.

Yet agriculture is not confined to any one item of grain or crop. Besides, agriculture is not the only activity that goes on in this world. If we compare man to an individual plant in a field, his role in relation to other phenomena of this world and universe should be perceivable, at least dimly. Coming back to agriculture, the farmer cultivates the land to grow food and other crops. That is his main aim. But he himself does not consume all the foodgrains he grows. As a matter of fact, it is likely that he does not use any part of his produce. Yet his agricultural operations are but a small part of the greater activity that is going on in this world. For his cultivation he needs the help and cooperation of many others—the soil, the climate, the seeds, the manure, the labour and machinery and so on. And we should also notice that his grain goes on transforming itself into so many of his other requirements. The money he gets from the sale of his produce he converts into his other requirements of life. After one harvest his operations do not cease. He repeats them every season and the same process repeats. But we have not been able to answer the one question, why this universe and its various auxiliaries exist?

Now if we assume God to be the great agriculturist (or should we call Him an agriculturist of agriculturists?) it will be clear how He cannot concern Himself exclusively with the welfare of individual human lives. I think this is a more or less plausible answer to the problem of suffering and pain. He has prepared the ground for each human being (as also all beings), yet every one of us does not assimilate the share of nourishment, spiritual or material, that is normally available to each. The lot of humanity springs from the same base and therefore the well or ill-being of any section thereof cannot be viewed in isolation. Suppose, as it happens in India, year after year monsoons fail, the cultivator cannot be blamed if the crops languish for want of water. I do understand that the analogy is not quite correct, because God the cultivator is also the One who sends the rain. God's laws appear as nature. But what I mean is the *common lot* of humanity in God's dispensation.

RELIGION—THE VITAL PART OF HUMANITY

Unlike helpless crops, man is endowed with the capacity to help each other (and also destroy each other!) The world is slowly moving towards a world government. It may take another century, or it may come sooner. All good things, great things are first born in the mind of man as far as his world is concerned. If we are to usher in the millennium, we have to make a start now. We have also to realise that religion has a vital part in every human activity, politics not excluded. "He who shall introduce into public affairs the principles of primitive Christianity will change the face of the world." Wrote Benjamin Franklin in the 18th century. Gandhi demonstrated this fact in his own life and in the history of his country. What is Christianity or any other religion, after all, if it is not the science of right living in conformity with God's known laws? The latest discoveries of science have proved that religion and philosophy are very much ahead of physical science. What the present day man wants to find out with proof after laborious research, our ancients guessed intuitively. We cannot wait to live our lives till all the elements of living, the various processes, have been convincingly proved to our satisfaction in the light of science. There need not be any conflict between science and religion. As already stated, since science tries to find out *how* a thing happens, religion assesses, or tries to assess, *why* things happen. They are complimentary to each other. Therefore we can and should introduce *science along with religion* into our universities, commercial and industrial institutions and governments.

If humanity can be one, why should a single Government for the whole world be impossible? The sun never used to set in the erstwhile British Empire. It was achieved through conquest, but the empire of humanity must now be consolidated by consent. Here is where the great nations of the world can demonstrate their wisdom. Let the leading democracies of the world try to form a federation, delegating, in stages, power to regulate the affairs of their individual countries. There is a great deal of ideology common between democratic countries like the United States, Canada, Great Britain, India, Australia, New Zealand and Japan. If a Common Market is possible for some of the European countries, a common government for the great countries above named should not be inconceivable. If Britain sought entry to the European Common Market realising its benefits, I do not despair about the possibilities of other nations seeking affiliation once they see the successful functioning of a common democratic government, thus leading to One-World Government. That is the only hope for mankind. It is not, I reiterate my firm belief, an isolated *political* question, We have seen a genuine desire born in the followers of world's great religions to appreciate and understand the greatness of other faiths. Let the political leaders seek sincerely the cooperation of religious leaders. Let religion enter the United Nations which is a political body. Did not the Pope grace the General Assembly and spoke from its platform? It is true that the United Nations has had its setbacks and shortcomings. That great Assembly of nations only reflects the imperfections of man. But we should not give up. We should resolve, like Ulysses, 'to strive, to seek, to find and not to yield.' *The kingdom of God which is within should manifest without too.* May God grant wisdom to man, and May He bless his efforts to build a new world. AMEN!

❑❑

27

EPILOGUE

After I concluded writing this book, I was thrilled to see an eminent scientist unexpectedly throw a flood of light in a sphere which is supposed to be not only not his, but also diametrically opposed to his calling. Dr. Warren Weaver's illuminating article, 'Can A Scientist Believe in God?' in the Reader's Digest* knocks the bottom out of the controversy over the possibility of co-existent faith in a personal God and the absolute, immanent, transcendent and impersonal Godhead which elucidates man's relationship or approach to the two aspects of the same reality. He has also unconsciously given substance to the theory of relative reality of illusion by drawing an analogy to the two different concepts of matter (one as energy in motion viewed by the atomic physicist and the other a solid object viewed like anyone of us). After reading that article of Dr. Weaver, I am happy to see the philosophy and religion which are the substratum of this book to be in tune with uptodate scientific knowledge and wholly compatible with it. Wisdom, divine wisdom is the monopoly of none. Knowledge multiplies when shared. The world has great need for it. In the twilight of overwhelming materialistic hedonism, the brilliant light of divine wisdom should be welcome from whichever direction it might irradiate. I thank the reader if he has read this book upto this stage; and if he has benefited, I humbly deny I have in any way laid him under debt. I am only the vehicle. Knowledge and wisdom are eternally existent. I fully believe in the common destiny of man and one day this knowledge and wisdom may become universally acknowledged as the only guide to right living.

❑❑

*I have taken the liberty of quoting a few passages from the article.

APPENDIX-A

A sense of rest, of deep quiet even. Silence within and without. A quietly-burning fire. A sense of comfort....I am not dazed or stupid, but only happy in this peaceful morning. Whatever may be the charm of emotion, I do not know whether it equals the sweetness of those hours of silent meditation, in which we have a glimpse and foretaste of the contemplative joys of Paradise. Desire and fear, sadness and care, are done away. Existence is reduced to the simplest form, the most ethereal mode of being, that is, to pure self-consciousness. It is a state of harmony, without tension and without disturbance, the dominical state of the soul, perhaps the state which awaits it beyond the grave. It is happiness as the Orientals understand it, the happiness of the anchorite, who neither struggles nor wishes any more, but simply adores and enjoys. It is difficult to find words in which to express this moral situation, for our languages can only render the particular and localised vibrations of life; they are incapable of expressing this motionless concentration, this divine quietitude, this state of the resting ocean, which reflects the sky, and is master of its own profundities. Things are then re-absorbed into their principles; memories are swallowed up in memory; the soul is only soul; and is no longer conscious of itself in its individuality and separateness. It is something which feels the universal life, a sensible atom of the Divine, of God. It no longer appropriates anything to itself, it is conscious of no void. Only the Yogis and Soufis perhaps have known in its profundity this humble and yet voluptuous state, which combines the joys of being and of non-being, which is neither reflection nor will, which is above both the moral existence and the intellectual existence, which is the return to unity, to the pleroma, the vision of Plotinus and of Proclus — Nirvana in its most attractive form.

It is clear that the western nations..... know very little of this state of feeling. For them life is devouring and incessant activity. They are eager for gold, for power, for dominion; their aim is to crush men and to enslave nature. They show an obstinate interest in means, and have not a thought for the end. They confound being with individual being and the expansion of the self with happiness — that is to say, they do not live by the soul; they ignore the unchangeable and the eternal; they live at the periphery of their being, because they are unable to penetrate to its axis. They are excited, ardent, positive, because they are superficial. Why so much effort, noise, struggle and greed? — it is all a mere stunning and defeaning of the self. When death comes they recognize that it is so — why not then admit it sooner? Activity is only beautiful when it is holy — that is to say, when it is spent in the service of that which passeth not away.

— AMIEL
(From his JOURNAL tr. by Mrs. Humphry Ward (Macmillan)
AMIEL, Henri Frederic. Swiss Philosopher and critic 1821-1881

❑❑

APPENDIX-B

All at once as it were, out of the intenseness of Consciousness of individuality, the individuality itself seemed to dissolve and fade away in boundless being, and this is not a confused state but the clearest of the clearest, the surest of the surest, the weirdest of the weirdest, utterly beyond words, where death was an almost laughable impossibility, the loss of personality the only true life.......

"I feel and know the flesh to be the vision, God and the spiritual to be the only real and true. Depend upon it, the spiritual is the real; it belongs to one more than the hand and foot.... you may tell me that my hand or my foot are only imaginary symbols of my existence, I could believe you but never, never can you convince me that the I is not the eternal reality and that the spiritual is not the true and real part of me."

—TENNYSON (Alfred Lord Tennyson)

A Memoir by his son (Macmillan)

❑❑

APPENDIX-C

ON THE BEING OF A GOD.

RETIRE;—The world shut out;—thy thoughts call home:—
Imagination's airy wing repress;—
Lock up thy senses;—let no passions stir;
Wake all to Reason—let her reign alone;
Then, in the soul's deep silence, and the depth
Of Nature's silence, midnight, thus inquire;
What am I? And from whence? I nothing know
But that I am; and, since I am, conclude
Something eternal: had there e'er been nought,
Nought still had been: Eternal there must be—
But what eternal? Why not human race,
And Adam's ancestors without an end?—
That's hard to be conceived; since ev'ry link
Of that long chain'd succession is so frail:
Can every part depend, and not the whole?
Yet grant it true; new difficulties rise;
I'm still quite out at sea; nor see the shore.
Whence earth, and these bright orbs?—Eternal too?
Grant matter was eternal; : still these orbs
Would want some other Father—much design
Is seen in all their motions, all their makes.
Design implies intelligence and art,
That can't be from themselves—or man; that art
Man scarce can comprehend could man bestow?
And nothing greater yet allow'd than man—

Who motion, foreign to the smallest grain
Shot through vast masses of enormous weight?
Who bid brute matter's restive lump assume?
Such various forms, and gave it wings to fly?
Has matter innate motion? Then each atom,
Asserting its indisputable right
To dance, would form a universe of dust.
Has matter none? Then whence shapeless and reposed?
Has matter more than motion? Has it thought,
Judgement, and genius? Is it deeply learn'd
In mathematics? Has it framed such laws,
Which, but to guess, a Newton made immortal?—
If art to from, and counsel to conduct,
And that with greater far than human skill,
Reside not in each block;—a GODHEAD reigns:-
And, if a GOD there is, that God how great!

— Edward Young (1681-1765)

❑❑

APPENDIX-D
PRAYER IS POWER

By Alexis Carrel, M.D.

Prayer is not only worship; it is also an invisible emanation of man's worshipping spirit — the most powerful form of energy that one can generate. The influence of prayer on the human mind and body is as demonstrable as that of secreting glands. Its results can be measured in terms of increased physical buoyancy, great intellectual vigour, moral stamina, and a deeper understanding of the realities underlying human relationships.

If you make a habit of sincere prayer, your life will be very noticeably and profoundly altered. Prayer stamps with its indelible mark our actions and demeanor. A tranquillity of bearing, a facial and bodily repose, are observed in those whose inner lives are thus enriched. Within the depths of consciousness a flame kindles. And man sees himself. He discovers his selfishness, his silly pride, his fears, his greeds, his blunder. He develops a sense of moral obligation, intellectual humility. Thus begins a journey of the soul toward the realm of grace.

Prayer is a force as real as terrestrial gravity. As a physician, I have seen men, after all other therapy has failed, lifted out of disease and melancholy by the serene effort of prayer. It is the only power in the world that seems to overcome the so-called "laws of nature"; the occasions on which prayer has dramatically done this have been termed "miracles." But a constant quieter miracle takes place hourly in the hearts of men and women who have discovered that prayer supplies them with a steady flow of sustaining power in their daily lives.

Too many people regard prayer as a formalized routine of words, a refuge for material things. We sadly undervalue prayer when we conceive it in these terms, just as we should underestimate rain by describing it as something that fills the birdbath in our garden. Properly understood, prayer is a mature activity indispensable to the fullest development of personality — the ultimate integration of man's highest faculties. Only in prayer do we achieve that complete and harmonious assembly of body, mind and spirit which gives the frail human reed its unshakable strength.

The words "Ask and it shall be given to you," have been verified by the experience of humanity. True prayer may not restore the dead child to life or bring relief from physical pain. But prayer, like radium, is a source of luminous, self-generating energy.

How does prayer fortify us with so much dynamic power? To answer this question (admittedly outside the jurisdiction of science), I must point out that all prayers have one thing in common. The triumphant hosannas of a great oratorio, or the humble supplication of an Iroquois hunter begging for luck in the chase, demonstrate the same truth; that human beings seek to augment their finite energy by addressing themselves to the infinite source of all energy. When we pray, we link ourselves with the inexhaustible motive power that spins the universe. We ask that a part of this power be apportioned to our needs. Even in asking, our human deficiencies are filled and we arise strengthened and repaired.

But we must never summon God merely for the gratification of our whims. We derive most power from prayer when we use it, not as a petition, but as a supplication that we may become more like him. Prayer should be regarded as practice of the presence of God. An old peasant was seated alone in the last pew of the village church. "What are you waiting for?" he was asked; and he answered, "I am looking at Him and He is looking at me." Man prays not only that God should remember him, but also that he should remember God.

How can prayer be defined? Prayer is the effort of man to reach God, to commune with an invisible being creator of all things, supreme wisdom, truth, beauty and strength, father and redeemer of each man. This goal of prayer always remains hidden to intelligence. For both language and thought fail when we attempt to describe God.

We do know, however, that whenever we address God in fervent prayer we change both soul and body for the better. It could not happen that any man or woman could pray for a single moment without some good result—"No man ever prayed", said Emerson, "without learning something."

One can pray everywhere. In the streets, the subway, the office, the shop, the school, as well as the solitude of one's room or among the crowd in a church. There is no prescribed posture, time or place.

"Think of God more often than you breathe, said Epictetus the Stoic. In order to really mould personality, prayer must become a habit. It is meaningless to pray in the morning and to live like a barbarian the remainder of the day. True prayer is a way of life, the truest life is literally a way of prayer.

The best prayers are like the improvisations of gifted lovers, always about the same thing yet never twice the same. We cannot all be as creative in prayer as Saint Theresa or Bernard of Clairvaux, both or whom poured their adoration into words of mystical beauty. Fortunately, we do not need their eloquence: our slightest impulse to prayer is recognized by God. Even if we are pitifully dumb, or if our tongues are overlaid with vanity or deceit, our meagre syllables of praise are acceptable to Him, and He showers us with strengthening manifestations of His love.

Today, as never before, prayer is a binding necessity in the lives of men and nations, The lack of emphasis on the religious sense has brought the world to the edge of destruction. Our deepest source of power and perfection has been left miserably undeveloped. Prayer, the basic exercise of the spirit, must be actively practiced in our private lives.

The neglected soul of man must be made strong enough to assert itself once more. For if the power of prayer is again released and used in the lives of common men and women; if the spirit declares its aim clearly and boldly, there is yet hope that our prayers for a better world will be answered.

❑❑

APPENDIX-E
THE SHEPHERD'S PRAYER

Moses saw a shepherd on the way, crying, "O Lord
Who choosest as Thou wilt,
Where art Thou, that I may serve Thee and sew
Thy shoon and comb Thy hair?
That I may wash Thy clothes and kill Thy lice and
Bring milk to Thee, O worshipful one;
That I may kiss Thy little hand rub Thy little
Feet and sweep Thy little room at bed-time."

On hearing these foolish words, Moses said,
"Man, to whom are you speaking?
What babble! What blasphemy and raving!
Stuff some cotton into your mouth!
Truly the friendship of a fool is enmity: the
High God is not in want of suchlike service."

The shepherd rent his garment, heaved a sigh,
And took his way to the wilderness.
Then came to Moses a Revelation: "Thou hast parted
My servant from Me.
Wert thou sent as a prophet to unite, or wert thou
Sent to sever?
I have bestowed on everyone a particular mode of worship,
I have given every one a peculiar form of expression.
The idiom of Hindustan is excellent for Hindus;
The idiom of Sind is excellent for the people of Sind.
I look not at tongue and speech, I look at the
Spirit and the inward feeling.
I look into the heart to see whether it be lowly,
Though the words uttered be not lowly.

Enough of phrase and conceits and metaphors!
 I want burning, burning; become familiar with that burning!
Light up a fire of love in thy soul, burn all
 Thought and expression away!
O Moses, they that know the conventions are of one sort,
 They whose souls burn are of another"..........

— Jalal-al-Din Rumi

❑❑

APPENDIX-F
ONE FOOT IN THE GRAVE

This indeed ought to be the constant exercise of the Christian life; it is fit for all times and for all persons, and without some degree of it, it is impossible to conquer the temptations of the world, or to live in the practice of divine and heavenly virtues. But this ought to be the constant business or entertainment rather, of those happy men who have lived long enough in the world to take a fair leave of it, who have run through all the scenes and stages of human life, and have now death and another world in view and prospect.

And it is this that makes a retirement from the world so necessary or very useful, not merely to ease our bodily labours, and to get a little rest from business, to dissolve in sloth and idleness, or to wander about to seek a companion, or to hear news, or to talk politics, or to find out some way to spend time, which now lies upon their hands, and is more uneasy and troublesome to them than business was. This is a more dangerous state, and does more indispose them for a happy death than all the cares and troubles of an active life; but we must retire from this world to have more leisure and greater opportunities to prepare for the next, to adorn and cultivate our minds and dress our souls like a bride who is adorned to meet her bridegroom.

When men converse much in this world and are distracted with the cares and business of it, when they live in a crowd of customers or clients, and are hurried from their shops to the Exchange or customs-house, or from their chambers to the bar, and when they have discharged one obligation and are so pressed hard by another, that at night they have hardly spirits left to say their prayers, nor any time for them in the morning, and the Lord's Day itself is thought more proper for rest and refreshment than devotion; I say, what dull cold apprehensions must such men have of another world! And after all the care we can take, how will this world inflame itself into our affections, when it employs our time and thoughts, when our whole business is buying and selling, driving good bargains, and making conveyances and settlements of estates? How will this disorder our passions, occasional feuds and quarrels, give us a tincture of pride, ambition, covetousness; there is work enough after a busy life, even for very good men, to wash out their stains and pollutions, and to get the taste and relish of this world out of their mouths, and to revive and quicken the sense of God and of another world.

This is a sufficient reason for such men, as I observed before, to think when it is time to leave off, and if not wholly to withdraw from the world, yet to contract their business, and to have the command of it, that they may have leisure to take care of their souls before they have so near a call and summons to Death; but much more necessary is it, when Death is even at the door, and by the course of Nature we know that it is so.

It is very proper to leave the world, before we are removed out of it, that we may know how to live without it, that we may not carry any hankerings after this world with us into tin next; and therefore it is very fitting, that there should be a *kind of middle state between this world and the next;* that is, that we should withdraw from this world, to wean ourselves from it, even while we are in it; which will make it more easy to part with this world, and make us more fit to go to the next. But it seems strangely undecent, unless the necessities of their families, or the necessities of the public call for it and exact it, to see men who are just a-going out of this world, who, it, may be, how as much under their riches, as under their age, plunging themselves over head and ears in this world, courting new honours and preferments with as much zeal as those who are but entering into the world. It is to be feared, such men think very little of another world, and will never be satisfied with earth till they are buried in it.

W. Sherlock — 'A Practical Discourse Concerning Death'

❑❑

28

BIBLIOGRAPHY

The Return to Religion — Dr. Henry C. Link

My Imitation of Christ — Thomas a Kempis

The Conquest of Happiness — Bertrand Russell

Rumi, Poet and Mystic — George Allen & Unwin, London

Meditations of Marcus Aurelius

Perennial Philosophy — Aldous Huxley

Key to Living — Mauriel Wrinch, Rider, London

The Psychology of Sex — Havelock Ellis

The Spectator — Joseph Addison

How to Win Friends and Influence People } Dale Carnegie
How to Stop Worrying and Start Living }

The Power of Positive Thinking — Dr. Norman Vincent Peale

Gandhi, the Man and His Mission — Louis Fischer

Lead Kindly Light — Vincent Sheean

My Gandhi — Dr. John Haines Holmes

A Journey to Lourdes — Dr. Alexis Carrel

War and Peace — Leo Tolstoy

Autobiography — Benjamin Franklin

Journal of AMIEL

Tennyson (Alfred Lord Tennyson) — A Memoir by his son, Macmillan

Marriage and Morals — Bertrand Russell

Author: Anchit Barnwal
Format: Paperback
Language: English
Pages: 168

Winners' Podium

Just as a winning podium can accommodate anyone on it each one of us is capable to be a winner, irrespective of our shortcomings and differences. Winners' Podium – Everyone Fits on it, attempts to do just that: make out a winner amongst each one of us.

This book offers elaborate guidelines for a balanced, successful and happy living. It tells how one can find his talent, attract ideas and be successful, both personally and professionally. It also talks of happiness and the steps to it.

Through stories, anecdotes, quotations, examples and day to day observations, this book can inspire you to not only attain that most desirable success, but also to hold on and grow both internally and externally with it.

Author: Aparna Chattopadhyay
Format: Paperback
Language: English
Pages: 184

What's Your Emotional IQ

This fascinating book authored by Dr. Aparna Chattopadhyay offers you a new vision of self-awareness which would enable you to assess your feelings, capabilities and aptitudes. As you develop self-awareness, you will not only be able to identify the emotional patterns in your life and will manage them well, but will also be able to activate all-round personality development.

This book enables you to:

- Generate fresh enthusiasm and ambition in your life
- Live more happily and effectively
- Build self-confidence and develop inner peace
- Enjoy better interper-sonal relationships
- Rid yourself of unwa-nted negative emotions